Antique Tins

IDENTIFICATION
& VALUES

BOOK III

Fred Dodge

COLLECTOR BOOKS

A Division of Schroeder Publishing Co., Inc.

The current values in this book should be used only as a guide. They are not intended to set prices, which vary from one section of the country to another. Auction prices as well as dealer prices vary greatly and are affected by condition as well as demand. Neither the author nor the publisher assumes responsibility for any losses that might be incurred as a result of consulting this guide.

Searching For A Publisher?

We are always looking for knowledgeable people considered to be experts within their fields. If you feel that there is a real need for a book on your collectible subject and have a large comprehensive collection, contact Collector Books.

Photography by Fred Dodge, Larry Manos, and Wm. Morford
Cover design by Michelle Dowling
Book design by Mary Ann Hudson

COLLECTOR BOOKS
P.O. Box 3009
Paducah, Kentucky 42002-3009

Copyright © 1999 by Fred Dodge

Printed in the U.S.A. by Image Graphics, Paducah, KY

...❖...

CONTENTS

...❖...

ACKNOWLEDGMENTS

I would like to thank the wonderful group of family, friends, collectors, and dealers listed below. Without their contributions of time, tins, and knowledge, this book would not be possible. With great hospitality, many have opened their homes to share their remarkable collections for all to enjoy.

Grant Smith (310) 454-5171

Alex & Marilyn Znaiden

Ken & Nancy Jones

Lehmann's Antique Adverstising & Collectibles
    Richard & Ann Lehmann (310) 253-3890
    Dealers — all advertising

Dave Garland (740) 376-0910
    Collector — shaving, specializing in Star

Michael & Sharon Hunt (317) 271-5602
    Dealers/Collectors — all advertising, popcorn

Bob & Correna Anderson (706) 657-8465
    Dealers/Collectors — all advertising, soda

Roy & Lynne Moseman (706) 549-0749

Arnold & Cindy Richardson

Schimpff's Confectionery (812) 283-8367
    Jill & Warren Schimpff
    347 Spring Street
    Jeffersonville, IN 47130
    Collectors/Museum — all candy memorabilia

Lawson & Lin Veasey

Buffalo Bay Auction Co. (612) 428-8480
    Larry & Sheri Manos
    5244 Quam Circle
    Rogers, MN 55374

Bob & Sherri Copeland

Carol Dodge

Jason Dodge

Don & Mary Perkins (317) 638-4519
    Collectors — all shaving memorabilia

Tom & Mary Lou Slike (216) 449-1913
    Collectors — all advertising, typewriter tins

Hoby & Nancy Van Deusen (860) 945-3456
    28 The Green
    Watertown, CT 06795
    Editor of Ribbon Tin News

Bill & June Mason (910) 738-1524

Allen & Judy Kimmel

Tom & Lynne Sankiewicz

Joan Bunte

Ed Houtz

David Morris & Steve Taylor

Mitch Morganstern

Wm. Morford Auctions (315) 662-7625
    William Morford
    RD#2
    Cazenovia, NY 13035

INTRODUCTION

Thank you for your interest in antique tins and for choosing to purchase this guide. You have joined a growing multitude of collectors searching for works from past artists. One does not need an explanation or reason to collect antique tins. The beautiful array of colors and artistic designs alone will explain the enormous demand for these exquisite collectibles. Year after year tins remain among the leading of investments. Some tins are purchases for as little as one dollar, while others require thousands. They are found in many unsuspecting places such as attics, trunks, closets, and even between walls of broken down estates. Tins have survived over the years because they were reused for organization, storage, and protection of other goods. Originally containing everything from perishable foods to office supplies, and depicting nearly every possible subject known, tins relate to almost every collector's desire. Enclosed you will find over 1,600 color photographs, many of which you may have never seen before. You will also find a descriptive and photo grading scale, values, sizes, companies, can markers, and information for finding antique tins. The values, assessed by many collectors or derived from past sales, may be advantageous to both novice and advanced collectors when purchasing tins. If you have not purchased my previous guides, *Antique Tins* and *Antique Tins, Book II*, I invite you to do so. Each guide contains hundreds of photographs other than the ones shown in Book III. I wish you great success and many pleasurable hours obtaining your collection.

PRICE AND CONDITION

The values within this guide were determined from countless hours of research and input from dealers, collectors, and owners of these tins. While viewing current market values from shows and auctions across the country, please keep in mind this is only a guide, and to pinpoint an exact value of a tin would be impossible due to the many different opinions and varying conditions. To a collector, price and condition are of upmost importance when purchasing a tin. Condition, rarity, and artistic design play major roles in determining a tin's value, but condition sometimes arouses controversy.

Many collectors have adopted the numeric grading system 1 through 10, with "1" being poor condition and "10" being mint. One collector may determine a tin grade 8, while another may disagree and consider it only grade 7. To help eliminate this confusion and different grading standards, I have tried to illustrate examples of this system on pages 7, 8, and 9.

It's important to remember if a tin merits a low grade, its value will drop drastically, but if its condition is pristine, it will most likely demand a higher price than that listed in this guide.

It has been my experience that very few collectors show interest in tins graded 6 or below. The majority of collectors would rather buy above grade 7 depending on its rarity, but many tins are scarce enough that collectors are overjoyed just to have an example of its kind added to their collection.

> NOTE: All values in this guide pertain to tins of grade 8 condition regardless of their appearance in these photographs. All containers are tin litho unless stated otherwise.

PRICING BRACKETS

Please understand, especially in the lower brackets, a tin valued at $10.00 will fall within the $1.00 – 25.00 bracket, but does not mean it will bring up to $25.00. A tin valued at $30.00 will fall within the $25.00 – 50.00 bracket, but does not mean it will or has ever commanded a $50.00 value. If a tin's condition is pristine, it may be worth the highest amount of the bracket or more, but not always.

Because of the many variables in condition and grading opinions, the purpose of these price brackets is to create flexibility and not pinpoint an exact value. Do not assume a $5.00 tin will sell for five times its value because it falls within the $1.00 – 25.00 price bracket.

$1.00 – 25.00	$300.00 – 350.00	$900.00 – 1,000.00
25.00 – 50.00	350.00 – 400.00	1,000.00 – 1,250.00
50.00 – 75.00	400.00 – 450.00	1,250.00 – 1,500.00
75.00 – 100.00	450.00 – 500.00	1,500.00 – 1,750.00
100.00 – 150.00	500.00 – 600.00	1,750.00 – 2,000.00
150.00 – 200.00	600.00 – 700.00	2,000.00 – 2,500.00
200.00 – 250.00	700.00 – 800.00	2,500.00 – 3,000.00
250.00 – 300.00	800.00 – 900.00	3,000.00+

No Price Available — I regret using this phrase, but after searching all available resources, I was unsuccessful in finding history or sales of these items. Most tins falling within this category are rare and have never been openly offered for sale, making it extremely difficult to determine their values. If the owners are not sure and cannot comment on the value of such items, it would be unfair for me to render a sole opinion. If these tins are available for sale in the future, it will be the decision of those performing the transactions as to where the value trends will begin.

SIZE

All measurements are rounded to the nearest ¼" and follow the order of height, width, and depth. Flat tins were photographed standing on their side, but measurements reflect the position of normal use. Canister measurements consist of height, then width through their diameter.

GRADING EXAMPLES

Grade 10: Mint – flawless – unused perfect condition – absolutely no sign of wear – rare to find tins in this condition.

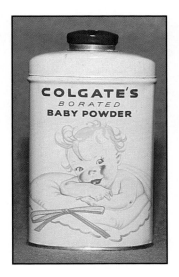

Grade 9: Excellent – near mint condition – nice luster – a few very minor scratches, paint flakes, or rub marks – no fading, dents, or rust.

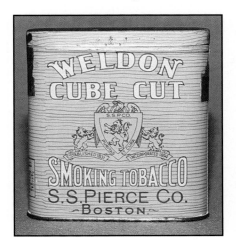

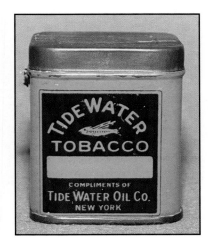

Grade 8: Fine – starting to show wear from minor scratches, flakes, or chips – possible minute pitting – displays very well – still highly collectible – no serious defects – no fading, dents, or rust.

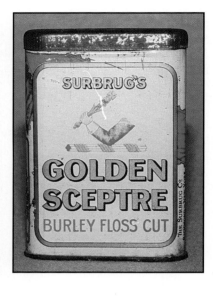

Grade 7: Good – beginning to show major problems – rough edges – several scratches, flakes, or rubs – medium pitting – possible light crazing – minute fading, rust, or dents – still shows with collectible quality.

3 Kings by Plain Tree Tobacco Co., England, 2½" x 5" x 3½", $1.00 – 25.00.

Ace High flat pocket by The Surbrug Co., marked Somers Bros., Brooklyn, New York, 1" x 4½" x 2½", $1,750.00 – 2,000.00. Courtesy of Grant Smith.

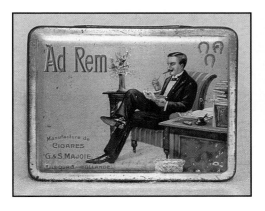

Ad Rem by G. & S. Majoie, Holland, ¾" x 4¼" x 3¼", $50.00 – 75.00. Courtesy of Grant Smith.

Adkin's Nut Brown store bin marked Imperial Tobacco Co. of Great Britian & Ireland, $100.00 – 150.00. Courtesy of Buffalo Bay Auction Co.

After Lunch snuff tin by Dodo Designs Manufacturers Ltd., London, England, ½" x 2½" x 2", $100.00 – 150.00. Courtesy of Buffalo Bay Auction Co.

Air Ship cigarette tin marked Imperial Japanese Government Monoply, 3¼" x 2½", $300.00 – 350.00. Courtesy of Grant Smith.

Air Ship cardboard vertical pocket with tin top and bottom by Globe Tobacco Co., Detroit, Michigan, 4" x 2¼" x 1", rare, no price available. Courtesy of Grant Smith.

Allen & Ginter Imperial by Allen & Ginter Tobacco Co., Richmond, Virginia, marked Ginna & Co. New York, 1¼" x 3¼" x 2½", $100.00 – 150.00. Courtesy of Grant Smith.

Allen & Ginter's American Tobacco Co., Successor, 2¼" x 3" x 2¼", $1.00 – 25.00.

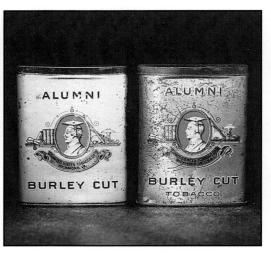

Alumni vertical pockets by United States Tobacco Co., Richmond, Virginia, 4" x 3" x 1", $1,000.00 – 1,250.00 ea.

Alvarez Lopez cigar tin, 5¼" x 5¼", $100.00 – 150.00. Courtesy of Buffalo Bay Auction Co.

Obverse

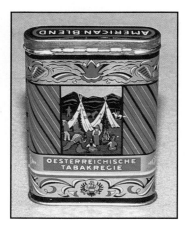

Reverse

American Girl flat pocket by Globe Tobacco Co., Detroit, Michigan, 1" x 4½" x 2½", $700.00 – 800.00. Courtesy of Grant Smith.

American Blend vertical pocket, American export for the German and Austrian market, 4½" x 3" x 1", rare, no price available.

Amorita by Buchanan & Lyall, marked S.A. Ilsley & Co., 1¾" x 4½" x 2½", $150.00 – 200.00. Courtesy of Grant Smith.

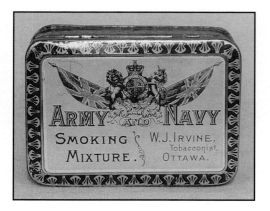

Army and Navy by W.J. Irvine, Ottawa, 2" x 5" x 3¾", $100.00 – 150.00. Courtesy of Grant Smith.

Army Club flat 50 cigarette tin, ¾" x 5¼" x 4½", $50.00 – 75.00.

Athlete by D. Ritchie Co., Montreal, Canada, marked Thos Davidson Mfg. Co., 1¾" x 5" x 3¾", $150.00 – 200.00. Courtesy of Grant Smith.

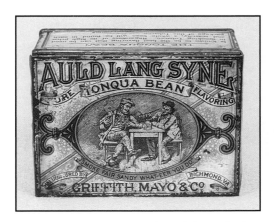

B.D.V. vertical pocket cigarette tin, 3" x 3½" x 1", $300.00 – 350.00. Courtesy of Grant Smith.

Auld Lang Syne by Griffith, Mayo & Co., Richmond, Virginia, marked Hasker & Marcus, 2¼" x 4½" x 3¼", $300.00 – 350.00. Courtesy of Grant Smith.

Azora cigar tin by Rothenberg & Schloss, $75.00 – 100.00. Courtesy of Buffalo Bay Auction Co.

Bambino vertical pockets by Bailey Bros. Inc., Winton-Salem, N.C., marked Tindeco, 4½" x 3" x 1", $1,250.00 – 1,500.00 ea. Courtesy of Bob & Sherri Copeland.

Barlow's Hand Made cigar tin by Barlow Cigar Co., Leavenworth, Kansas, marked A.C. Co.50A, 5½" x 6" x 4", $25.00 – 50.00. Courtesy of Bob and Sherri Copeland.

Bears' Medium by Imperial Tobacco Co. of New Zealand Ltd., Wellington, ¾" x 3¼" x 2¼", $25.00 – 50.00. Courtesy of Grant Smith.

Beeswing marked Ogdens, England, American Tobacco Co. Successor, 1" x 4¾" x 3¼", $100.00 – 150.00. Courtesy of Grant Smith.

Belle Fair cigar canister marked A. Schulte, Ritter Can Co., Philadelphia, 5½" x 5½", $100.00 – 150.00.

Ben Bey, 2¾" x 9¼" x 6½", $75.00 – 100.00. Courtesy of Buffalo Bay Auction Co.

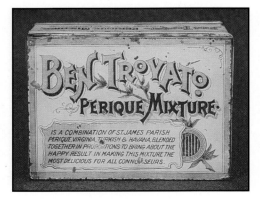

Ben Trovato by W.T. Hancock, marked Hasker & Marcuse, Richmond, Virginia, 2" x 4¼" x 3¼", $100.00 – 150.00. Courtesy of Grant Smith.

Benson & Hedges flat 50 cigarette tin by Benson & Hedges, New York, ½" x 5¾" x 4½", $50.00 – 75.00. Courtesy of Bob & Sherri Copeland.

Berta Gravely vertical box by Gravely & Miller Tobacco Co., marked Hasker & Marcuse, 4½" x 3½" x 2", $3,000.00+. Courtesy of Grant Smith.

Bingo flat pocket by The United States Tobacco Co's., Richmond, Virginia, ½" x 3¾" x 2¼", $800.00 – 900.00. *Courtesy of Grant Smith.*

Bishop's Move flat pocket by Cohen & Weenen Co., London, ¾" x 3¼" x 2¼", $50.00 – 75.00.

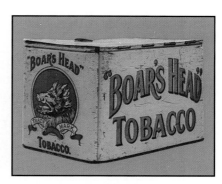

Blue Boar by American Tobacco Co., 4¼" x 4¼", $25.00 – 50.00.

"Boars Head" British tin, 6" x 9" x 5½", $75.00 – 100.00. *Courtesy of Buffalo Bay Auction Co.*

Black Fox cigar canister by McLeod Nolan, London, Canada, marked MacDonald, 5¼" x 5¼", $600.00 – 700.00. *Courtesy of Grant Smith.*

Boldt's Specials cigar flat pocket by Waldorf-Astoria Segar Co's., New York, ¾" x 3¼" x 5½", $75.00 – 100.00. *Courtesy of Richard & Ann Lehmann.*

Bob White by Marburg Bros., marked Ginna & Co., 3½" x 4" x 2½", $250.00 – 300.00.

Bremer Flagge by C.F. Vogelsang, Bremen, 1" x 4¼" x 3¼", $50.00 – 75.00. Courtesy of Grant Smith.

Bright American Falcon Birdseye vertical box by Kinney Bros. Tobacco Co., 4¾" x 3¼" x 2", rare, no price available. Courtesy of Grant Smith.

Brink-Dolan vertical pocket marked Factory No. 93, 1st Dist. of Missouri, 4½" x 3" x 1", rare, no price available.

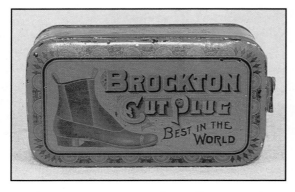

Brockton marked Somers Bros., Brooklyn, New York, 1½" x 4½" x 2½", $150.00 – 200.00. Courtesy of Grant Smith.

Brooklyn Eagle marked Somers Bros., Brooklyn, New York, 2" x 4½" x 3¼", $450.00 – 500.00. Courtesy of Grant Smith.

Brown Bear paper label vertical pocket by Hall & Lyon Co. of New England, 2½" x 3½" x 1", $75.00 – 100.00. Courtesy of Bob & Sherri Copeland.

Bumper cardboard with tin top and bottom by Spaulding & Merrick, Chicago, Illinois, 6½" x 4½" x 4½", $400.00 – 450.00. Courtesy of Grant Smith.

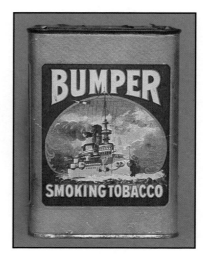

C.A.A. Mixture marked Somers Bros., Brooklyn, New York, 2¼" x 4½" x 3¼", $250.00 – 300.00. Courtesy of Grant Smith.

California Nugget flat pocket by The American Tobacco Co., 1" x 4½" x 2¾", $75.00 – 100.00. Courtesy of Grant Smith.

Camerettes flat cigar pocket by Cameron & Cameron, ¾" x 3¼" x 1¾", $100.00 – 150.00. Courtesy of Grant Smith.

Cameron's Bright Long Cut, 1½" x 3½" x 2¼", $100.00 – 150.00. Courtesy of Grant Smith.

Cameron's Havelock by British-Austalasian Tobacco Co. Proprietary Ltd., Melbourne, Australia, 2½" x 3¼" x 2¼", $100.00 – 150.00. Courtesy of Grant Smith.

Cameron's Light Pressed by Cameron & Cameron, Richmond, Virginia, marked Hasker & Marcuse, 1¼" x 4½" x 3¼", $200.00 – 250.00. Courtesy of Grant Smith.

Canuck by Cameron & Cameron, Richmond, Virginia, 1½" x 4½" x 2¾", $25.00 – 50.00.

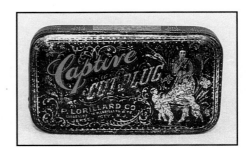

Captive flat pocket by P. Lorillard Co., Jersey City, New Jersey, ¾" x 4½" x 2½", rare, no price available. Courtesy of Grant Smith.

Catac by Cameron & Cameron, Richmond, Virginia, marked Hasker & Marcuse, Richmond, Virginia, 2" x 4" x 3", $75.00 – 100.00. Courtesy of Grant Smith.

Central Union lunch box by The United States Tobacco Co., Richmond, Virginia, 5¼" x 7½" x 4½", $100.00 – 150.00. Courtesy of Allen & Judy Kimmel.

Check by Rock City Cigar Co. Ltd., Livis, Quebec, marked Whittall Can Co., 5" x 5¼", $150.00 – 200.00. Courtesy of Richard & Ann Lehman.

Checkers by Weisert Bros. Tobacco Co., St. Louis, left: 4½" x 3" x 1", $500.00 – 600.00; center: 6" x 5", $450.00 – 500.00; right top: 4" x 3½" x 1", $400.00 – 450.00; right bottom: 5" x 6" x 4", $500.00 – 600.00. Courtesy of Grant Smith.

Chicago Cubs by Rock City Tobacco Co., Quebec, 3¼" x 6", $75.00 – 100.00.

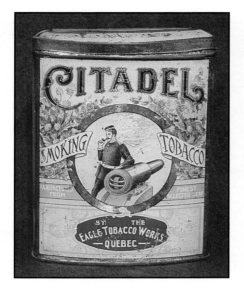
Obverse

Reverse

Citadel by Eagle Tobacco Works, Quebec, 6¼" x 5" x 4", $700.00 – 800.00. Courtesy of Grant Smith.

Cleveland Centennial Mixture by Cameron & Cameron, Richmond, Virginia, 2½" x 5½" x 3", rare, no price available. Courtesy of Grant Smith.

Club Room vertical box by J.B. Pace Tobacco Co., marked Somers Bros., 4¾" x 3½" x 2", rare, $3,000.00+. Courtesy of Grant Smith.

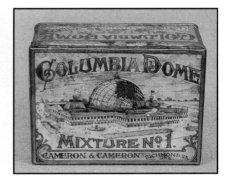

Columbia Dome by Cameron & Cameron, Richmond, Virginia, 2¼" x 4½" x 3¼", rare, $3,000.00+. Courtesy of Grant Smith.
Note: Another variation exists with Mixture No. 2.

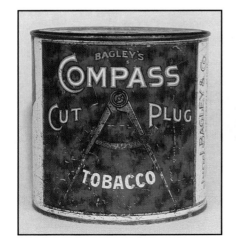

Compass by John J. Bagley & Co., Detroit, Michigan, marked A.C. Co. 70A, 5¼" x 5¼", $100.00 – 150.00. Courtesy of Grant Smith.

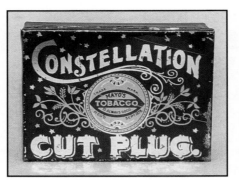

Conroy, Mike paper label cigar canister, 5" x 5¼", $200.00 – 250.00. Courtesy of Buffalo Bay Auction Co.

Constellation by P.H. Mayo & Bros. Inc., Richmond, Virginia, 1½" x 4½" x 3¼", $100.00 – 150.00. Courtesy of Grant Smith.

Continental Can Co. promotional example tin by Continental Can Co., 3" x 2¼" x 1", $25.00 – 50.00.

Coronet by Frank Jones, New York, marked Somers Bros., 2" x 4½" x 2½", $75.00 – 100.00. Courtesy of Grant Smith.

Coronet Navy Cut paper label by Cameron & Cameron Co., 3" x 2½", $75.00 – 100.00.

Country Life by H.D. & H.O. Wills, Sydney, Australia, ¾" x 3½" x 3", $25.00 – 50.00. Courtesy of Grant Smith.

Court House by The R.M. Jenkinson Co., Pittsburgh, Pennsylvania 2¾" x 6" x 4", $250.00 – 300.00. Courtesy of Grant Smith.

Creme de la Creme by J.M. Fortier, Montreal, Canada, 2" x 5" x 3½", $200.00 – 250.00. Courtesy of Grant Smith.

Cupid Bouquet flat pocket by Buchner Tobacco Co., New York, ¼" x 3½" x 3¼", $75.00 – 100.00.

Dandy Fifth by Salmon & Gluckstein, London, 1½" x 5½" x 3", $50.00 – 75.00. Courtesy of Ken & Nancy Jones.

Defender marked Factory No. 16, 2nd Dist. New York, 3" x 3¾" x 2½", $200.00 – 250.00. Courtesy of Grant Smith.

Desert Gold, 1¼" x 3¼", $25.00 – 50.00. Courtesy of Grant Smith.

Decision by Baer-Wolf Co., Cleveland, Ohio, 1½" x 5" x 4½", $1.00 – 25.00.

Detroit Club by Charles J. Holton, Detroit, Michigan, left: 4" x 2¼" x 1½"; center: 3¾" x 3½" x 1"; right: 3½" x 3½" x 1"; $1,500.00 – 1,750.00 ea.

Desert Gold cardboard with tin top and bottom by National Tobacco Co. Ltd., Port Ahuriri, 7" x 4¼", $100.00 – 150.00. Courtesy of Grant Smith.

Diamond flat pocket by Charles W. Allen, Chicago, ½" x 3½" x 2¼", $250.00 – 300.00. Courtesy of Grant Smith.
Note: Reverse is Try Darey & Joan Plug.

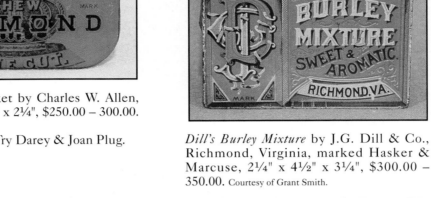

Dill's Burley Mixture by J.G. Dill & Co., Richmond, Virginia, marked Hasker & Marcuse, 2¼" x 4½" x 3¼", $300.00 – 350.00. Courtesy of Grant Smith.

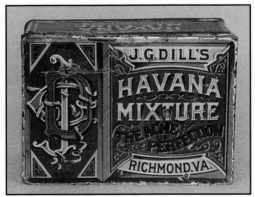

Dill's Havana Mixture by J.G. Dill & Co., Richmond, Virginia, marked Hasker & Marcuse, 2¼" x 4½" x 3¼", $300.00 – 350.00. Courtesy of Grant Smith.

Dill's Natural Leaf by J.G. Dill & Co., Richmond, Virginia, marked Hasker & Marcuse, 1¼" x 4½" x 3¼", $200.00 – 250.00. Courtesy of Grant Smith.

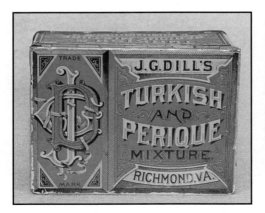

Dill's Turkish and Perique by J.G. Dill & Co., Richmond, Virginia, marked Hasker & Marcuse, 2¼" x 4½" x 3¼", $300.00 – 350.00. Courtesy of Grant Smith.

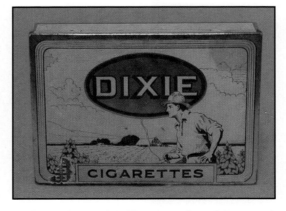

Dixie by Imperial Tobacco Co., Montreal, Canada, 1¼" x 5¾" x 4¼", $100.00 – 150.00.

Dixie Queen marked Factory No. 2 Dist. of Maryland, 6½" x 4¼", $350.00 – 400.00. Courtesy of Grant Smith.

Dixie Queen marked Hasker & Marcuse, Richmond, Virginia, 6½" x 5", $350.00 – 400.00. Courtesy of Grant Smith.

Donniford paper label vertical pocket by Christian Peper Tobacco Co., 4¼" x 3¼" x 1¼", $50.00 – 75.00.

Drawing Room by P. Lorillard & Co., Jersey City, New Jersey, 2½" x 3" x 2½", $75.00 – 100.00. Courtesy of Grant Smith.

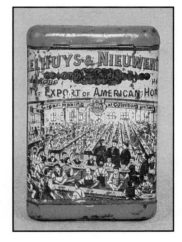

Dresselhuys & Nieuwenhuysen vertical pocket marked specialty export of American Home Cigars, 4¾" x 3" x 1", rare, no price available. Courtesy of Grant Smith.

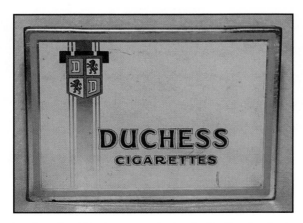

Duchess flat 50 cigarette tin by L.O. Grothe Ltd., Montreal, ¾" x 5¾" x 4¼", $25.00 – 50.00. Courtesy of Bob & Sherri Copeland.

Dutch Heerenbaai-Tobak paper label by Theodorus Niemeijer Ltd., Holland, U.S. Distributor- Holland Dutch Pipe Co., New York, 2¾" x 2¾", $25.00 – 50.00.

Duke's Mixture store bin by W. Duke Sons & Co., marked Ginna & Co., 18½" x 11¾" x 9¼", $1,500.00 – 1,750.00. Courtesy of Grant Smith.

Eagle flat pocket by American Tobacco Co., ½" x 3¼" x 1¾", $250.00 – 300.00. Courtesy of Grant Smith.

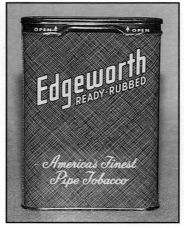

Edgeworth vertical pocket by Larus & Brother Co., Inc., Richmond, Virginia, 4¼" x 3" x 1", rare, no price available. Courtesy of Edward Seidel.

Edgeworth paper label by Larus & Brother Co. Inc., Richmond, Virginia, 5" x 5", $1.00 – 25.00.

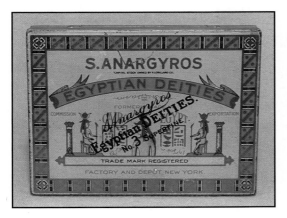

Egyptian Deities flat 50 cigarette tin by S. Anargyros owned by P. Lorillard Co., ¾" x 5¼" x 4¼", $25.00 – 50.00.

El Marino J.T.D., 1" x 5" x 3", $50.00 – 75.00.
Courtesy of Grant Smith.

El Parmela marked Factory No. 57
11th Dist. Ohio, Heekin Can Co.,
5¼" x 3½" x 1½", $100.00 – 150.00.

El Producto, 5¾" x 5½", $150.00 – 200.00. Courtesy of Buffalo Bay Auction Co.

El Retina flat cigar tin marked Factory No. C-6, 8th Dist. Missouri, 1¼" x 5" x 3½", $25.00 – 50.00.

El Trebow paper label, 5½" x 4¼", $75.00 – 100.00. Courtesy of Buffalo Bay Auction Co.

El Verdaro vertical cigar box, 5" x 3¼" x 3¼", $150.00 – 200.00. Courtesy of Wm. Morford Auctions.

El Verso by Deisel-Wenmer Co., Lima, Ohio, 1½" x 5" x 2¼", $1.00 – 25.00.

Elcho by Elcho Cigar Co., Boston, Massachusetts, 2½" x 5¼" x 3¼", $100.00 – 150.00.

Ethel Barrymore by Hatterman Bros. Co., Louisville, Kentucky, 1" x 8" x 1¾", $1.00 – 25.00.

Every Day flat pocket by Nall & Williams Tobacco Co., Louisville, Kentucky, ¾" x 4½" x 2½", $300.00 – 350.00. Courtesy of Grant Smith.

F-F vertical pocket by Frishmuth Bro. & Co. Inc., Philadelphia, 4½" x 3" x 1", rare, no price available. Courtesy of Grant Smith.

Famosa by Cameron & Cameron, Richmond, Virginia, marked S.A. Ilsley, 2¼" x 4½" x 3¼", $150.00 – 200.00. Courtesy of Grant Smith.

Federal Judge vertical cigar box, 5½" x 3½" 3½", $100.00 – 150.00. Courtesy of Buffalo Bay Auction Co.

Fifth Avenue paper label marked 1st Dist. of Missouri, 5" x 3½" x 3½", $1.00 – 25.00.

Fischer's paper label vertical pocket by Fischer's Pipe Shop, Boston, Massachusetts, 3" x 3½" x 1", $25.00 – 50.00. Courtesy of Bob & Sherri Copeland.

Floating Cloud by J.G. Flint Jr. & Co., Milwaukee, marked Norton Bros., Chicago, 2¾" x 4½" x 3¼", $200.00 – 250.00. Courtesy of Grant Smith.

Flor de Odin paper label vertical box, 5¾" x 3" x 3", $100.00 – 150.00. Courtesy of Buffalo Bay Auction Co.

Floral Gem by Moen Tobacco Co., Newark, New Jersey, marked S.A. Ilsley & Co., Brooklyn, New York, ¼" x 3¼" x 3", $75.00 – 100.00.

Florida flat pocket by Spaulding & Merrick, Chicago, Illinois, ½" x 3¾" x 2¼", $900.00 – 1,000.00. Courtesy of Grant Smith.

Forest Hill paper label vertical pocket by Louis Klein Cigar Co., Cleveland, Ohio, 4" x 3½" x 1", $25.00 – 50.00. Courtesy of Bob and Sherri Copeland.

Foursome Mixture by The Robert Sinclair Tobacco Co. Ltd., London & Newcastle, 1" x 4¼" x 3¼", $200.00 – 250.00. Courtesy of Grant Smith.

Friendship flat pocket by D.H. McAlpin & Co's., marked Hasker & Marcuse, 1" x 4½" x 2½", $150.00 – 200.00. Courtesy of Grant Smith.

Gallaher's by Gallaher Ltd., ¾" x 3¾" x 1¾", $50.00 – 75.00. Courtesy of Grant Smith.

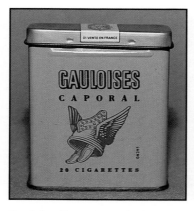

Garcia Smokers cigar tin marked Cakildow Maker, Bethesda, Ohio, 5" x 4", $25.00 – 50.00. Courtesy of Tom & Mary Lou Slike.

Gauloises French vertical pocket cigarette tin, 3" x 2½" x 1¼", $50.00 – 75.00.

Gibson Girl cigarettes cases marked Manoli Berlin, top left: vertical pocket 3" x 3¼" x ¾", $350.00 – 400.00; bottom left: box 1½" x 4¼" x 3", $75.00 – 100.00; right: flat pocket ½" x 3" x 2¾", $100.00 – 150.00. Courtesy of Bob and Sherri Copeland.

Gold Bell by The Rock City Tobacco Co., Quebec, 1½" x 5" x 3¾", $75.00 – 100.00. Courtesy of Grant Smith.

Gold Coin by Buchner Tobacco Co., New York, ¾" x 3¼" x 2¼", $1,000.00 – 1,250.00. Courtesy of Grant Smith.

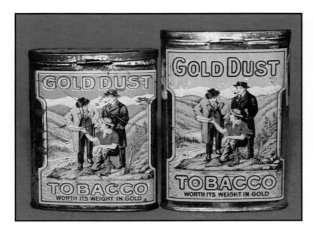

Gold Dust vertical pockets by The B. Houde Co. Ltd., Quebec, Canada, left: 4" x 3" x 1", $3,000.00+; right: 4½" x 3" x 1", $2,500.00 – 3,000.00. Courtesy of Ed Houtz.

Gold Leaf vertical box by John Lemesurier, Quebec, 6½" x 4½" x 3¼", $100.00 – 150.00. Courtesy of Grant Smith.

Golden Butterfly by T.C. Williams Co., Richmond, Virginia, marked Ginna & Co. New York, 2¾" x 5" x 3", $400.00 – 450.00. Courtesy of Grant Smith.

Golden Crest by Monopol Tobacco Works, New York, 2¾" x 5" x 3", $150.00 – 200.00. Courtesy of Grant Smith.

Golden Eagle flat pocket by T.C. Williams Co., ¾" x 3¼" x 2¼", $150.00 – 200.00. Courtesy of Grant Smith.

Golden Square Mixture by Cameron & Cameron, Richmond, Virginia, marked Hasker & Marcuse, 2¼" x 4½" x 3¼", $200.00 – 250.00. Courtesy of Grant Smith.

Greek Slave marked 6th Dist. of Virginia, 2¼" x 4½" x 3¼", $700.00 – 800.00. Courtesy of Grant Smith.

Golden Leaf by B. Houde & Co., Quebec, Canada, marked MacDonald Mfg. Co., 6¾" x 4" x 4", $50.00 – 75.00.

Green Turtle Selects by Gordon Cigar & Cheroot Co. Inc., 4½" x 6" x 3¾", $1,250.00 – 1,500.00. Courtesy of Grant Smith.

Hamilton Harris vertical cigar box by Hamilton Harris and Co's., Indianapolis, Indiana, marked National Can Co., 5½" x 3¼" x 3¼", $75.00 – 100.00. Courtesy of Bob & Sherri Copeland.

Hand Made Stogie Pantelas vertical cigar box, 6" x 4" x 4", $25.00 – 50.00.

Happy Hit by Sam H. Harris Co., Chicago, Illinois, marked Hasker & Marcuse, Richmond, Virginia, 1¾" x 4½" x 2¾", rare, no price available. Courtesy of Grant Smith.

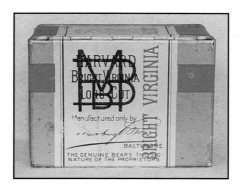

Harmony paper label by Liggett & Myers Tobacco Co., 3¼" x 2¾", $50.00 – 75.00.

Harvard Bright Virginia by Marburg Bros., Baltimore, Maryland, 2¼" x 4½" x 3¼", $200.00 – 250.00. Courtesy of Grant Smith.

Harvest King vertical cigar box marked A.C. Co. 50A, 5¾" x 4¼" x 4¼", $100.00 – 150.00. Courtesy of Grant Smith.

Havana Sticks embossed cigar box, 5¾" x 3½" x 3½", $25.00 – 50.00. Courtesy of Buffalo Bay Auction Co.

Hayward Mixture paper label vertical pocket by Moss & Lowenhaupt, St. Louis, 4" x 3½" x 1", $25.00 – 50.00. Courtesy of Bob and Sherri Copeland.

Hiawatha by Daniel Scotten & Co., Detroit, Michigan, marked Ginna & Co., 2½" x 5" x 3", left: $75.00 – 100.00; right: $100.00 – 150.00.

High Admiral, 1½" x 3", $100.00 – 150.00. Courtesy of Grant Smith.

Hignett's Cavalier Brand by Hignett Bros. Co., Branch of Imperial Tobacco Co. of Great Britian, 2½" x 7¼" x 3¼", $75.00 – 100.00. Courtesy of Grant Smith.

Hip-Poc cigar vertical pocket by Lee Roy Myers Co., 5½" x 3" x 1", rare, $600.00 – 700.00.

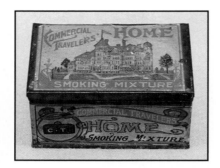

Home paper label by Daniel Scotten & Co., Detroit, Michigan, 2" x 4" x 2½", $75.00 – 100.00. Courtesy of Grant Smith.

Hot Scotch paper label vertical pocket by Falk Tobacco Co., Richmond, Virginia, 4" x 2½" x 1¼", rare, $250.00 – 300.00. Courtesy of Bob & Sherri Copeland.

Huia by Nelson Tobacco Co. Ltd., ¾" x 4¼" x 4¼", $75.00 – 100.00. Courtesy of Grant Smith.

Huntleigh paper label by Christian Peper Tobacco Co., 5" x 3½" x 3½", $1.00 – 25.00.

Huntoon and Gorhams marked Ginna & Co., New York, 1¼" x 4½" x 3¼", $100.00 – 150.00. Courtesy of Grant Smith.

Hyman's Mixture marked Somers Bros., Brooklyn, New York, 2½" x 4½" x 3¼", rare, no price available. Courtesy of Grant Smith.

Idolita by Jose Escalante & Co., Tampa-New Orleans-Chicago, 4½" x 5½", $1.00 – 25.00. Courtesy of Bob and Sherri Copeland.

Imperial Alliance by Imperial Tobacco Co. of New Zealand Ltd., Wellington, 1" x 3½", $25.00 – 50.00. Courtesy of Grant Smith.

Imperial Bird's Eye by Allen & Ginter, Richmond, Virginia, American Tobacco Co. Successor, 4½" x 3¼" x 2", $200.00 – 250.00. Courtesy of Grant Smith.

Imperial Cube Cut by Allen & Ginter's, 3" x 2", $1.00 – 25.00. Courtesy of Bob & Sherri Copeland.

Imperial Ruby by T.C. Williams Co., Virginia, 1" x 3¼" x 2¼", $1.00 – 25.00. Courtesy of Grant Smith.

Indian cigar tin marked Manuel Fernandez Habana, 1" x 5" x 3½", $200.00 – 250.00. Courtesy of Wm. Morford Auctions.

Island vertical box by Daniel Scotten & Co., Detroit, Michigan, marked Ginna & Co., 4¾" x 3½" x 2", $900.00 – 1,000.00. Courtesy of Grant Smith.

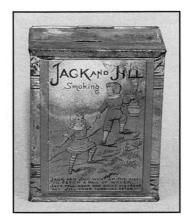

Jack & Jill paper label vertical box by Wm. S. Kimball & Co., 4½" x 3½" x 2", $700.00 – 800.00. Courtesy of Grant Smith.

John Ruskin by Lewis Cigar Mfg. Co., Newark, New Jersey, 5½" x 3½" x 3½", $100.00 – 150.00. Courtesy of Ken & Nancy Jones.
Note: Two variations exist, with and without 5¢.

John's Trade Mark paper label by John's Pipe Shop, Los Angeles, California, 3" x 3½" x 1", $50.00 – 75.00. Courtesy of Buffalo Bay Auction Co.

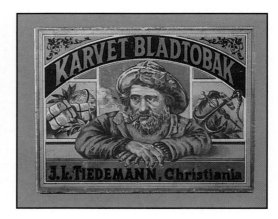

Judge Wright by J.C. Newman Cigar Co., Cleveland Ohio, 5½" x 3½" x 3½", $150.00 – 200.00. Courtesy of Buffalo Bay Auction Co.

Kadee vertical pocket by Christian Peper Tobacco Co., St. Louis, Missouri, 4½" x 3" x 1", $1,000.00 – 1,250.00. Courtesy of Grant Smith.

Karvet Bladtobak by J.L. Tiedemann, Christiania, 1" x 5" x 4", $100.00 – 150.00. Courtesy of Buffalo Bay Auction Co.

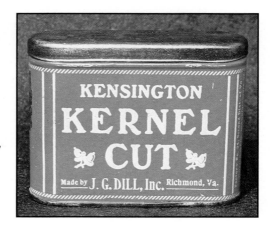

Kensington vertical pocket by J.G. Dill Inc., Richmond, Virginia, 2¾" x 3½" x 1¼", $700.00 – 800.00. Courtesy of Allen & Judy Kimmel.

Kenway, 5" x 5¼", $25.00 – 50.00. Courtesy of Buffalo Bay Auction Co.

Key West cigar canister marked Liberty Can Co., 5¼" x 4¼", $100.00 – 150.00. Courtesy of Richard & Ann Lehman.

King Dutch by I. Brudno & Sons, 5" x 6¼" x 4¼", $100.00 – 150.00. Courtesy of Richard & Ann Lehmann.

King of All by A.H. Motley Co., Reidsville, North Carolina, 1½" x 3½" x 2¼", rare, no price available. Courtesy of Grant Smith.

Kipawa cigar vertical box marked Heekin Can Co., Cincinnati, Ohio, 6½" x 4½" x 4½", $450.00 – 500.00. Courtesy of Alex & Marilyn Znaiden.

Kopper Kettle Klub cigar canister by Joseph Weinreich, Dayton, Ohio, 5½" x 5", $200.00 – 250.00. Courtesy of Grant Smith.

La Belle Creole (Turkish & Perique mixture) by S. Hernshein Bros. & Co., New Orleans, Louisiana, 2¼" x 6" x 4", $200.00 – 250.00. Courtesy of Grant Smith.

La Corona cigar canister, 5¼" x 5", $75.00 – 100.00. Courtesy of Richard & Ann Lehmann.

La Preferencia by Eugene Vallens & Co., marked Havana-American Co. Successor, Subsidiary of the American Tobacco Co., 5" x 3¾", $200.00 – 250.00.

La Primadora oval cigar tin, 5¾" x 5½" x 4¾", $100.00 – 150.00. Courtesy of Buffalo Bay Auction Co.

La Resta flat cigar box, 1½" x 5¼" x 3¾", $25.00 – 50.00.

La Teresa paper label cigar tin marked 11th Dist. of Maryland, $1.00 – 25.00.

Lane's Eringold flat pocket by Larus & Bros., Co. Inc., ½" x 3¼" x 2¼", $1.00 – 25.00.

Le Roy vertical pocket by L. Miller & Sons, New York, 4½" x 3½" x 1¼", $150.00 – 200.00. Note: Another variation exists without 25¢ button.

Liberty Mixture by Gravely & Miller, Danville, Virginia, marked Hasker & Marcuse, 2¼" x 4½" x 3¼", rare, no price available. Courtesy of Grant Smith.

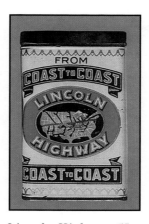

Lincoln Highway, 5" x 3¼" x 3¼", $100.00 – 150.00. Courtesy of Buffalo Bay Auction Co.

Little Morton vertical cigar box, 4½" x 3" x 3", $150.00 – 200.00. Courtesy of Wm. Morford Auctions.

Lone Hand flat pocket by John Weisert Tobacco Co., marked A.C. Co. 50A, ¾" x 3¼" x 1¾", $200.00 – 250.00. Courtesy of Grant Smith.

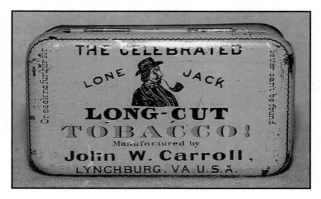

Lone Jack by John W. Carroll, Lynchburg, Virginia, 1½" x 4¾" x 2¾", $25.00 – 50.00.

Lord Tennyson Canadian cigar tin, 5" x 5", $100.00 – 150.00. Courtesy of Wm. Morford Auctions.

Louis Dobbelmann's flat pocket by Louis Dobbelmann, Rotterdam, ¾" x 3" x 2¼", $100.00 – 150.00.

Lucky Strike by British-American Tobacco Co. Ltd., marked made in U.S.A., 3" x 2½" x 1", $500.00 – 600.00.

Lucy Hinton by The British-Australasian Tobacco Co., Melbourne, Australia, 3¼" x 3¼" x 2¼", $1.00 – 25.00. Courtesy of Grant Smith.

Luxor Royale by Continental Cigarette Co., ¾" x 3¼" x 2¾", $25.00 – 50.00. Courtesy of Grant Smith.

Luxura vertical pocket by Booker Tobacco Co., Lynchburg, Virginia, 4" x 3½" x 1", $3,000.00+. Courtesy of Grant Smith.

MacDonald's Kilty Brand by MacDonald & Co., Glasgow, ½" x 3¼" x 1½", $25.00 – 50.00. Courtesy of Grant Smith.

Madeira flat pocket by W.J. Yarbrough & Sons, marked Hasker & Marcuse, 1" x 4½" x 2½", $300.00 – 350.00. Courtesy of Grant Smith.

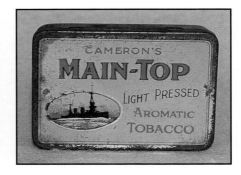

Main Top (Cameron's) by British-Australasian Tobacco Co. Ltd. Proprieter, Melbourne, Australia, 1" x 3¼" x 2¼", $25.00 – 50.00. Courtesy of Grant Smith.

Maji paper label vertical pocket by J.L. Liesenberg, Mason City, Iowa, 3¾" x 3" x 1", $50.00 – 75.00. Courtesy of Grant Smith.

Mal-Kah No. 3 flat 50 cigarette tin by Mah-Kah Cigarette Co. Ltd., England, ¾" x 5½" x 4", $50.00 – 75.00.

Matoaka by Patterson Bros. Tobacco Corp.,
Richmond, Virginia, 4½" x 6¼" x 4¼",
$1,000.00 – 1,250.00. Courtesy of Grant Smith.

Maryland Club store bin, 15" x 10" x 7",
$1,000.00 – 1,250.00. Courtesy of Tom & Mary Lou Slike.

Meerschaum horizontal box, 3¾" x
5" x 3½", $50.00 – 75.00. Courtesy of
Buffalo Bay Auction Co.

Mayo's Mixture by P.H. Mayo & Bro. Inc.,
Richmond, Virginia, marked Ginna & Co.,
New York, 2" x 4½" x 3¼", $100.00 –
150.00. Courtesy of Grant Smith.

Mick McQuaid by P.J. Carroll &
Co. Ltd., ¾" x 3¼" x 2", $25.00
– 50.00. Courtesy of Grant Smith.

Mellow Smoke flat pocket by Moore & Calvi,
New York, marked Hasker & Marcuse, 1" x
4½" x 2½", $100.00 – 150.00. Courtesy of Grant Smith.

Mick McQuaid by P.J. Carroll & Co. Ltd., 1½" x 7½" x 3¼", $50.00 – 75.00. Courtesy of Grant Smith.

Miller's vertical cigar box, 5¾" x 3½" x 3½", $75.00 – 100.00. Courtesy of Buffalo Bay Auction Co.

Mohawk Chief by The Charles Co., York, Pennsylvania, marked Liberty Can Co., Lancaster, Pennsylvania, 5½" x 6" x 4¼", $1,500.00 – 1,750.00. Courtesy of Grant Smith.

Monopol (Turkish tobacco) by Monopol Tobacco Works, New York, marked Ginna & Co., New York, ¾" x 3" x 1¾", $200.00 – 250.00. Courtesy of Grant Smith.

Monopol London Club by Monopol Tobacco Works, New York, 4¾" x 3½" x 2", $1,250.00 – 1,500.00. Courtesy of Grant Smith.

Monopole (Turkish & Russian) by European Model Tobacco Works, Joseph Huppmann Proprieter, New York, marked Ginna & Co., New York, 1¼" x 4" x 2½", $100.00 – 150.00. Courtesy of Grant Smith.

Monopole (Turkish Tobacco) by Joseph Huppmann Proprieter, New York, marked Ginna & Co., New York, ¾" x 3" x 1¾", $200.00 – 250.00. Courtesy of Grant Smith.

Montan-Union marked Ges. Gesch, 6" x 6" x 4", $50.00 – 75.00. Courtesy of Buffalo Bay Auction Co.

Motley's Best by A.H. Motley Co., Reedsville, North Carolina, 2" x 4½" x 3¼", $300.00 – 350.00. Courtesy of Grant Smith.

My Ladies by J.W. Collins & Co., Richmond, Virginia, ¼" x 3½" x 3¼", $75.00 – 100.00.

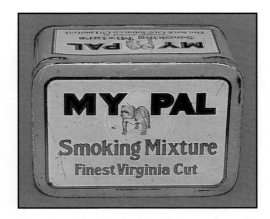

My Pal by The Rock City Tobacco Co., 3" x 5" x 3½", $50.00 – 75.00. Courtesy of Grant Smith.

Namona by L. Miller & Sons, New York, marked Hasker & Marcuse, 2½" x 5" x 3", $100.00 – 150.00. Courtesy of Grant Smith.

Natural Tobacco No. 40 by J.W. Boisvert, St. Boniface, Quebec, Canada 4¾" x 3¾" x 2½", $25.00 – 50.00. Courtesy of Richard & Ann Lehmann.

Navy Scotch Snuff paper label by Geo. W. Helm Co., New Jersey, 2½" x 2", $1.00 – 25.00.

Nebraska Blossom by Heacock Cigar Co., 5¼" x 5½", $2,500.00 – 3,000.00. Courtesy of Wm. Morford Auctions.
Note: A less valuable paper label variation exists.

Nestor Gianaclis cigarette tin by Nester Gianaclis Ltd., Cairo, Egypt, ½" x 3½" x 3, $25.00 – 50.00. Courtesy of Grant Smith.

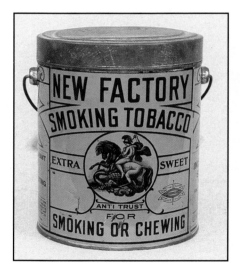

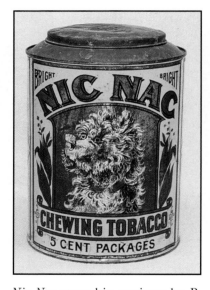

No. 10 Cut Plug, 1¼" x 3¼", $25.00 – 50.00. Courtesy of Grant Smith.

New Factory pail by Independent Snuff Co. Manufacturers, Chicago, marked C.C. Co., 7" x 5½", $200.00 – 250.00. Courtesy of Grant Smith.

Nic Nac store bin canister by B. Leidersdorf Co., 12" x 8¼", $1,250.00 – 1,500.00. Courtesy of Grant Smith.

No. 10 Cut Plug by National Tobacco Co. Ltd., 6" x 4½", $75.00 – 100.00. Courtesy of Grant Smith.

No. 3 Toasted Navy Cut, 1¼" x 3¼", $50.00 – 75.00. Courtesy of Grant Smith.

O.K. Canadian tin by L. Larue Jr., 2" x 5" x 3½", $50.00 – 75.00. *Courtesy of Buffalo Bay Auction Co.*

North Star by Cotterill Fenner & Co., Dayton, Ohio, marked Ginna & Co., left: 1¾" x 4½" x 3¼", $500.00 – 600.00; right: ½" x 2¼" x 3½", $400.00 – 450.00. *Courtesy of Grant Smith.*

No. 3 Toasted Navy Cut cardboard with tin top and bottom by National Tobacco Co. Ltd., Port Ahuriri, 7" x 4½", $150.00 – 200.00. *Courtesy of Grant Smith.*

Ogden's by Imperial Tobacco Co. of Canada, 4" x 4½", $1.00 – 25.00. *Courtesy of Bob and Sherri Copeland.*

Old Abe flat pocket by B. Leidersdorf & Co., marked Somers Bros., ½" x 3½" x 2¼", $1,500.00 – 1,750.00. *Courtesy of Grant Smith.*

Old Briar by United States Tobacco Co., Richmond, Virginia, 1½" x 5½" x 4", $1.00 – 25.00. Note: Several sizes exist.

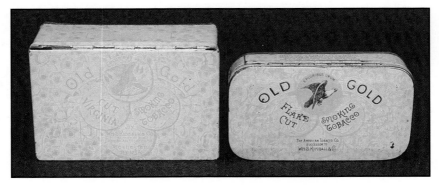

Old Gold by The American Tobacco Co. Successor to Wm. S. Kimball & Co., left: 2" x 4½" x 3"; right: 1" x 4½" x 2½"; $50.00 – 75.00 ea. *Courtesy of Grant Smith.*

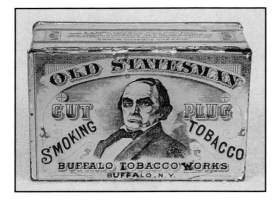

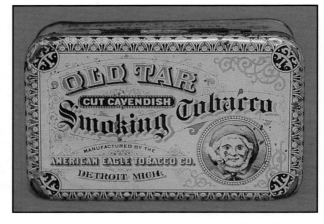

Old Statesman by Buffalo Tobacco Works, Buffalo, New York, marked Somers Bros., 2" x 4½" x 3", $600.00 – 700.00. Courtesy of Grant Smith.
Note: Another variation by S.F. Hess & Co. exists.

Old Tar by American Eagle Tobacco Co., Detroit, Michigan, 2½" x 6" x 4", $200.00 – 250.00. Courtesy of Grant Smith.

OPM (Our Private Mixture) left: by Cobb, Bates & Yerxa Co., 4½" x 3" x 1", $300.00 – 350.00; right: by S.S. Pierce Co., Boston, Massachusetts, 4¼" x 3" x 1", $250.00 – 300.00.

Orchid vertical box by Frishmuth Bros., marked F.S. Towel Co., New York-Germany, 4¼" x 3¼" x 3¼", $300.00 – 350.00. Courtesy of Grant Smith.

O'San by P & H Cigar Co., Red Lion, Pennsylvania, 5" x 5¼", $250.00 – 300.00. Courtesy of Wm. Morford Auctions.

Osmundo cigar tin, 1¾" x 5" x 3¼", $25.00 – 50.00. Courtesy of Buffalo Bay Auction Co.

Our Chums Slice flat pocket, ¾" x 3¼" x 1¾", $75.00 – 100.00. Courtesy of Grant Smith.

OU paper label, $50.00 – 75.00.
Courtesy of Buffalo Bay Auction Co.

Our Key West marked Somers Bros., Brooklyn, New York, 2¼" x 4½" x 3¼", $250.00 – 300.00. Courtesy of Grant Smith.

Our Special Mixture paper label vertical pocket by Isaacson's Cigar Store, Denver, 3¼" x 3" x 1", $50.00 – 75.00. Courtesy of Grant Smith.

Par Excellence marked Somers Bros., 2¼" x 4½" x 3¼", $250.00 – 300.00. Courtesy of Grant Smith.

Pastora by Elwood Myers Co., Springfield, Ohio, 5¾" x 5" x 5", $100.00 – 150.00. Courtesy of Wm. Morford Auctions.

Perfection by Dudgeon & Arnell Proprieter, Melbourne, Australia, ½" x 3½" x 2¼", $25.00 – 50.00. Courtesy of Grant Smith.

Peter Hauptmann & Co's Mixture by Peter Hauptmann & Co., St. Louis, Missouri, 2" x 4" x 3", $100.00 – 150.00. Courtesy of Grant Smith.

Peter Stuyvesant vertical cigarette pocket by American Cigarette Co. (overseas) Ltd., 3¾" x 2¼" x 1", $1.00 – 25.00.

Phenix by Nestor Gianaclis Ltd., ¾" x 4½" x 2¾", $25.00 – 50.00. Courtesy of Grant Smith.

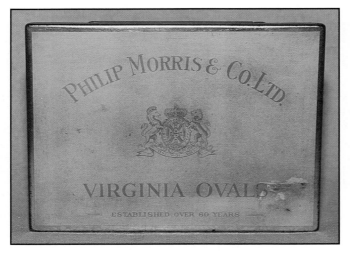

Pickwick Club by The Griffith, Mayo Manufacturing Co., Richmond, Virginia, 1½" x 4" x 2½", $600.00 – 700.00. Courtesy of Grant Smith.

Philip Morris flat 50 cigarette tin, Tucket Tobacco Co. Ltd. Successor, ¾" x 5¾" x 4¼", $25.00 – 50.00. Courtesy of Bob & Sherri Copeland.

Pioneer by Eagle Tobacco Co., Quebec, 1¾" x 5" x 3½", $100.00 – 150.00. Courtesy of Grant Smith.

Player's Navy Cut by H.D. & H.O. Wills, 1" x 3½", $25.00 – 50.00. Courtesy of Grant Smith.

Plug Crumb Cut vertical pocket by David P. Ehrlich Co., Boston, Massachusetts, 4¼" x 3½" x 1", $250.00 – 300.00.

Pom Pom by John H. Swisher & Son, Newark, Ohio, ¾" x 4" x 2¼", $1.00 – 25.00.

Post Office by E. Ablel, marked Somers Bros., Brooklyn, New York, 2¼" x 4½" x 3¼", $1,250.00 – 1,500.00. Courtesy of Grant Smith.

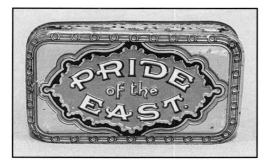

Pride of the East by The United States Tobacco Co., Richmond, Virginia, 1" x 4½" x 2½", $100.00 – 150.00. Courtesy of Grant Smith.

Pride of Virginia flat pocket by J. Wright Co., ¾" x 4½" x 2¾", $1.00 – 25.00.

Prince de Monaco by Ed. Laurens, Alexandrie, ½" x 3¼" x 2¾", $25.00 – 50.00. Courtesy of Grant Smith.
Note: Another variation exists.

Princeton Mixture vertical box by Marburg Bros., Baltimore, Maryland, marked Somers Bros., 4½" x 3½" x 2", $400.00 – 450.00. Courtesy of Grant Smith.

Prize Crop by Stephen Mitchell & Son, ¾" x 4¼" x 3¼", $1.00 – 25.00. Courtesy of Grant Smith.

Prize Winners by Chas C. Wells, Binghamptom, New York, 1¾" x 4¾" x 3", $100.00 – 150.00. Courtesy of Grant Smith.

Pure Perique by Surbrug Co., New York, 1½" x 3¼" x 2½", $25.00 – 50.00. Courtesy of Mike & Sharon Hunt.

Purity by Cameron & Cameron, Richmond, Virginia, marked Hasker & Marcuse, 1¼" x 4½" x 3¼", $350.00 – 400.00. Courtesy of Grant Smith.

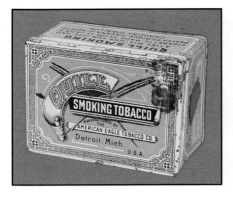

Quill by American Eagle Tobacco Co., Detroit, Michigan, 2¼" x 4½" x 3¼", $150.00 – 200.00.

Raleigh cigarette tin by Brown & Williamson Tobacco Corp., Louisville, Kentucky, 3¼" x 2¾", $25.00 – 50.00.

Ram's Horn by Gravely & Miller Co., Danville, Virginia, marked Hasker & Marcuse, 1¾" x 4½" x 2½", $250.00 – 300.00. Courtesy of Grant Smith.

Reception by American Eagle Tobacco Co., Detroit, Michigan, marked S.A. Ilsley & Co., New York, 4" x 4" x 2¼", rare, no price available. Courtesy of Grant Smith.

Red Funnel by Zimmer & Co. Inc., Petersburg, Virginia, ½" x 3¼" x 2¼", $300.00 – 350.00. Courtesy of Grant Smith.

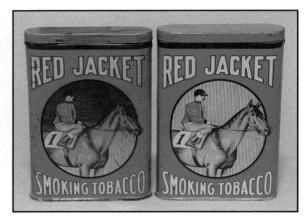

Red Jacket vertical pockets by B. Payne's Sons Tobacco Co., Albany, New York, 4½" x 3" x 1"; left: metalic background, rare, no price available; right: $75.00 – 100.00. Courtesy of Bob & Sherri Copeland.
Note: The left tin has a tax stamp, unusual for this tin.

Red-White-Blue marked Heekin Can Co., Cincinnati, Ohio, 5¼" x 7¾" x 5", $75.00 – 100.00. Courtesy of Tom & Mary Lou Slike.

Reise-begleiter cigarette tin, ¾" x 4¾" x 4", $1.00 – 25.00.

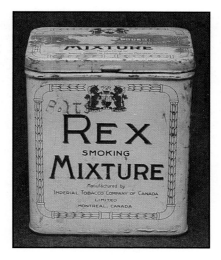

Rex vertical box by Imperial Tobacco Co., Montreal, Canada, 4¾" x 4" x 2½", $1.00 – 25.00.

Richmond Golden Leaf by Richmond Cavandish Co., Liverpool, 1½" x 4½" x 3½", $500.00 – 600.00. Courtesy of Grant Smith.

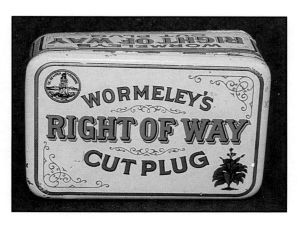

Right of Way by The Wormeley Co., 2½" x 6" x 4", $250.00 – 300.00. Courtesy of Grant Smith.

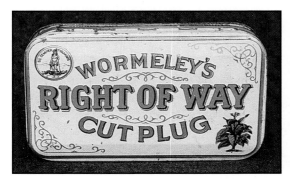

Right of Way by The Wormeley Co., 1" x 2½" x 4¼", rare, no price available. Courtesy of Grant Smith.

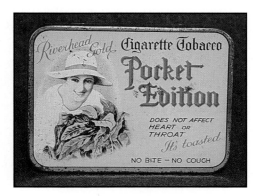

Riverhead Gold pocket edition by National Tobacco Co. Ltd., Napier, ¾" x 4¼" x 3¼", $25.00 – 50.00. Courtesy of Grant Smith.

Riverhead Gold by National Tobac-co Co. Ltd., Napier, 1¼" x 3¼", $25.00 – 50.00. Courtesy of Grant Smith.

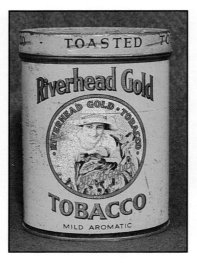

Riverhead Gold by National Tobacco Co. Ltd., 6" x 4½", $100.00 – 150.00. Courtesy of Grant Smith.

Robert Burns flat cigar box by Straiton & Storm, New York, 1" x 4½" x 3¾", $50.00 – 75.00.

Rooster paper label by The United States Tobacco Co., Nashville, Tennessee, 2¼" x 1¾", $1.00 – 25.00.

Roth-Handle vertical pocket cigarette tin, 3¾" x 2¼" x 1", $25.00 – 50.00.

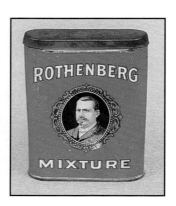

Rothenberg vertical pocket by Rothenberg & Schloss, 4¼" x 3" x 1", $500.00 – 600.00. Courtesy of Grant Smith. Note: A shorter variation exists.

Royal Club by J. Lemesurier & Sons, Quebec, marked MacDonald, 2¼" x 5" x 3½", $250.00 – 300.00. Courtesy of Grant Smith.

Royal Diadem by S.F. Hess & Co., Rochester, New York, marked Hasker & Marcuse, Richmond, Virginia, 1¾" x 4" x 2½", $500.00 – 600.00. Courtesy of Grant Smith.

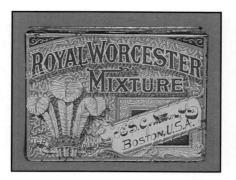

Royal Worcester by E.S. Goulston & Co., Boston, marked Hasker & Marcuse, Richmond, Virginia, 1¾" x 4½" x 3¼", $400.00 – 450.00. Courtesy of Grant Smith.

Rummie vertical pocket by Knickerbocker Tobacco Co., New York, New York, 4½" x 3" x 1", $600.00 – 700.00.

Russian Cigarette Tobacco by Aug. Beck & Co., Chicago, 2¼" x 4½" x 3¼", $100.00 – 150.00. Courtesy of Grant Smith.

S & M's Special by Sichel & Mayer, Portland, Oregon, marked S.A. Ilsley, 1¾" x 4½" x 3¼", $250.00 – 300.00. Courtesy of Grant Smith.

Saffa by Saffa Manufacturers, St. Louis, 1¾" x 5" x 3", $150.00 – 200.00. Courtesy of Grant Smith.

Sam's Own by Samuel Gawith & Co. Ltd., 1" x 4¼" x 3¼", $25.00 – 50.00. Courtesy of Grant Smith.

Samsoun by Imperial Turkish Tobacco & Cigarette Co., marked Somers Bros., Brooklyn, New York, 2¼" x 4½" x 3¼", $1,000.00 – 1,250.00. Courtesy of Grant Smith.

Sarajevo flat pocket by G.A. Georgopula & Co., New York, ¼" x 3¼" x 2¾", $1.00 – 25.00.

Scotch Snuff by Larkin & Morrill, Byfield, Massachusetts, 2¼" x 1½", $1.00 – 25.00. Courtesy of Bob & Sherri Copeland.

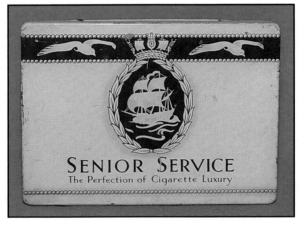

Senior Service flat 50 cigarette tin by J.A. Pennsylvaniattreiouex Ltd., England, ¾" x 5¾" x 4¼", $50.00 – 75.00. Courtesy of Bob & Sherri Copeland.

Senoussi marked Reemtsma Manufacturers of Oriental Cigarettes, ¾" x 4¼" x 2¾", $25.00 – 50.00. Courtesy of Grant Smith.

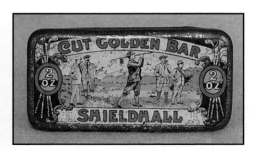

Sensation by P. Lorillard Co., 6½" x 5", $100.00 – 150.00. Courtesy of Bob & Sherri Copeland.

Serdar Turmac by Turkish-Macedonian Tobacco Co., ¾" x 4" x 3", $50.00 – 75.00. Courtesy of Grant Smith.

Shieldhall (Golden Bar) (2oz.) by Scottish Co-Operative Wholesale Society Ltd. Tobacco Factory, ¾" x 3¾" x 2", $100.00 – 150.00. Courtesy of Grant Smith.

Shieldhall (Heath) by Scottish Co-Operative Wholesale Society Ltd. Tobacco Factory, ½" x 3¼" x 2½", $50.00 – 75.00. Courtesy of Grant Smith.

Shogun by E.O. Eshelby Tobacco Co., Cincinnati, Ohio, left: 4¾" x 5½" x 3"; right: vertical pocket, 4½" x 3" x 1"; rare, $3,000.00+ ea. Courtesy of Grant Smith.

Siegel's paper label vertical pocket by Siegel Bros. Inc., Cleveland, Ohio, 3" x 3½" x 1", $25.00 – 50.00.

Shubs vertical pocket by Shubs Tobacco Co. Inc., Philadelphia, Pennsylvania, 4½" x 3" x 1", $1,000.00 – 1,250.00. Courtesy of Ed Houtz.

Silver Bell by The Rock City Tobacco Co., marked Mac-Donald Mfg. Co., Toronto, Canada, 2" x 3" x 3", $75.00 – 100.00. Courtesy of Buffalo Bay Auction Co.

Silver Fern by Dominion Tobacco Co. Ltd., Wellington, ¾" x 4¼" x 3¼", $25.00 – 50.00. Courtesy of Grant Smith.

Ski-Hi paper label cigar canister, 5½" x 5¼", $2,500.00 – 3,000.00. Courtesy of Wm. Morford Auctions.

Skiff flat pocket by Samuel Gawith, Kendal, England, 1" x 4½" x 3¼", $25.00 – 50.00.

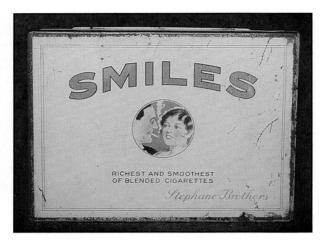

Smiles flat 50 cigarette tin by Stephano Bros., ¾" x 5¾" x 4¼", $200.00 – 250.00. Courtesy of Bob & Sherri Copeland.

Snap Shots vertical pockets by Falk Tobacco Co., left: 4¼" x 3½" x 1", $500.00 – 600.00; right: 4" x 3" x 1", rare, no price available. Courtesy of Bob & Sherri Copeland.

Spana-Cuba by Yocum Bros., marked Liberty Can Co., 5¼" x 3½" x 3½", $25.00 – 50.00. Courtesy of Buffalo Bay Auction Co.

Sportsman Canadian flat 50 cigarette tin marked Continental Can Co., ¾" x 5¾" x 4¼", $1.00 – 25.00.

Squatter by Cameron & Cameron, Richmond, Virginia, 2¼" x 4½" x 2¾", $50.00 – 75.00.

St. James by Cameron & Cameron, Richmond, Virginia, 2½" x 5½" x 3", $150.00 – 200.00. Courtesy of Grant Smith.

St. James Parish Perique by H. Mandelbaum, New York, marked Hasker & Marcuse, Richmond, Virginia, 1½" x 4" x 2¾", rare, no price available. Courtesy of Grant Smith.

St. Leger by D. Ritchie Co., Montreal, Canada, 2" x 4" x 3¾", $100.00 – 150.00. Courtesy of Grant Smith.

Stag by P. Lorillard & Co., Jersey City, New Jersey, left: 6¼" x 5" x 5"; right: 4½" x 3½" x 2", $200.00 – 250.00 ea. Courtesy of Grant Smith.

Star flat pocket by J.G. Flint Jr., Milwaukee, ½" x 3½" x 2¼", $450.00 – 500.00. Courtesy of Grant Smith.

Star Five by Julius Fecht, Ottumwa, Iowa, $100.00 – 150.00. Courtesy of Buffalo Bay Auction Co.

Sterling store bin canister by Spaulding & Merrick, Liggett & Myers Successor, 11½" x 8¼", $200.00 – 250.00. Courtesy of Grant Smith.

Strause's paper label by Strause Cigar Stores, Peoria, Illinois, 4" x 2½" x 1½", $100.00 – 150.00.
Note: A litho version exists.

Sullivan Powell British tin by Sullivan Powell & Co., 6" x 3" x 1½", $50.00 – 75.00. Courtesy of Buffalo Bay Auction Co.

Summer-Time cardboard canister with tin top and bottom by Spaulding & Merrick Tobacco Co., Liggett & Myers Successor, 6" x 5¼", $75.00 – 100.00.

Sun Beam by J.G. Dill, Richmond, Virginia, marked Hasker & Marcuse, 1¾" x 4½" x 2½", $500.00 – 600.00. Courtesy of Grant Smith.

Sun Cured by John J. Bagley & Co., Detroit, Michigan, marked A.C. Co. 70A, 5½" x 5¾", $350.00 – 400.00. Courtesy of Grant Smith.

Sunset Trailers cigar canister, 5" x 5", $450.00 – 500.00. Courtesy of Grant Smith.

Sweet Crop paper label by Cohen Weenen & Co. Ltd., London, England, 2¼" x 2¾", $1.00 – 25.00.

Tallman Stogies cigar canister, marked Tindeco, 6¼" x 5", $450.00 – 500.00. Courtesy of Grant Smith.

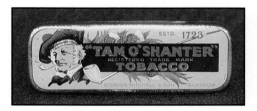

Tam O' Shanter by Stephen Mitchell & Son, Glasgow, ¾" x 3¼" x ¾", $25.00 – 50.00. Courtesy of Grant Smith.

Tanagra cigarette vertical pocket marked Ed Laurens, Alexandie-Le Caire (Egypt), 3" x 3¼" x ¾", $200.00 – 250.00.

Tasman by Dominion Tobacco Co. Ltd., Wellington, ¾" x 3¼" x 2¼", $25.00 – 50.00. Courtesy of Grant Smith.

Taxi vertical pockets by Imperial Tobacco Co., 4¼" x 3" x 1", $3,000.00+ each.
Note: Another variation exists without the word tobacco.

Temple Bar by British-Australasian Tobacco Co., Ltd. Proprieter, Melbourne, Australia, ¾" x 3¼" x 2¼", $50.00 – 75.00. Courtesy of Grant Smith.

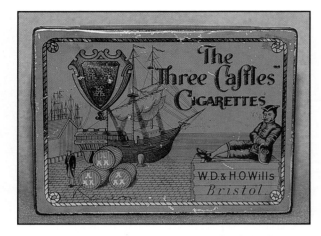

The Doctor, 5½" x 3½" x 3½", $300.00 – 350.00.
Courtesy of Buffalo Bay Auction Co.

Three Castles flat 50 cigarette tin by W.D. & H.O. Wills, Bristol, marked Imperial Tobacco Co., Ltd., ¾" x 5¾" x 4¼", $75.00 – 100.00. Courtesy of Bob & Sherri Copeland.

Three States by Harry Weissinger Tobacco Co., American Tobacco Co. Successor, ¾" x 4½" x 2¾", $250.00 – 300.00. Courtesy of Wm. Morford Auctions.

Three Feathers, 5¼" x 6" x 3¾", $350.00 – 400.00.
Courtesy of Grant Smith.

Tide Water (complimentary) by Tide Water Oil Co., New York, 2½" x 2¼" x 2¼", $100.00 – 150.00.

Tiger cardboard store bin with tin top and bottom by P. Lorillard Co., Jersey City, New Jersey, 11" x 8" x 6¼", $100.00 – 150.00.
Courtesy of Buffalo Bay Auction Co.

Tiger Brand by Tiedemanns, ¾" x 4¼" x 2¼", $100.00 – 150.00. Courtesy of Grant Smith.

Tiger blue lunch box by P. Lorillard Co., Jersey City, New Jersey, 8" x 7½" x 5½", $100.00 – 150.00. Courtesy of Buffalo Bay Auction Co.

Top by R.J. Reyonlds Co., Winston-Salem, North Carolina, 3¾" x 5¼", $1.00 – 25.00.

Tom Keene paper label by Bondy & Lederer, New York, 5¼" x 4½" x 2½", $25.00 – 50.00.

Topaz by W.W. Russell, 2¼" x 4½" x 3¼", $250.00 – 300.00. Courtesy of Grant Smith.

Tortoise Shell marked Factory No. 2 Dist. of Maine, 1" x 3" x 2", $100.00 – 150.00. Courtesy of Grant Smith.

Totem paper label on wood cigar box by Waitt & Bond Inc., Boston, Massachusetts, 5¼" x 5½" x 6½", $100.00 – 150.00. Courtesy of Grant Smith.

Tuckett's Orinoco flat pocket by Geo. E. Tuckett & Son Co., 1" x 5" x 3¾", $75.00 – 100.00.

Turf Blue Label by Carreras Ltd., London, England, ½" x 3¾" x 2¾", $50.00 – 75.00. Courtesy of Grant Smith.

Turkish Tobacco by Cameron & Cameron Co., Richmond, Virginia, 1¼" x 4½" x 3¼", $350.00 – 400.00. Courtesy of Grant Smith.

Turmac by Turkish-Macedonian Tobacco Co., Amsterdam-Zurich-Bruxelles, ¾" x 4¾" x 3", $25.00 – 50.00. Courtesy of Grant Smith.

Two Belles cigar tin, 1¼" x 5½" x 3½", $100.00 – 150.00. Courtesy of Buffalo Bay Auction Co.

Two Eleven by Estabrook & Eaton, Boston, 1" x 4" x 3", $75.00 – 100.00. Courtesy of Grant Smith.

Two Eleven vertical pocket by Estabrook & Eaton, Boston, 4" x 3" x 1", $700.00 – 800.00. Courtesy of Bob & Sherri Copeland.

U.S. flat pocket by United States Tobacco Co., marked Hasker & Marcuse, 1" x 4½" x 2½", rare, no price available. Courtesy of Grant Smith.

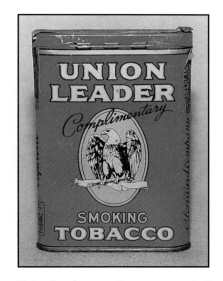

U.S. Marine basketweave design lunch box, 4" x 7" x 5", $25.00 – 50.00.

Union Leader complimentary vertical pocket by P. Lorillard Co., 4½" x 3" x 1", $100.00 – 150.00. Courtesy of David Morris.

United Hand Made paper label marked Factory No. 1 5th Dist. New Jersey, 5¼" x 3¼" x 3¼", $25.00 – 50.00. Courtesy of Bob & Sherri Copeland.

University of Chicago by Cameron & Cameron, Richmond, Virginia, 2¼" x 4½" x 3¼", rare, no price available. Courtesy of Grant Smith.

University of Michigan by American Eagle Tobacco Co., Detroit, Michigan, marked S.A. Ilsley & Co., New York, 4" x 3¾" x 2¼", $200.00 – 250.00. Courtesy of Grant Smith.

Velvet Smokarols cardboard by Liggett & Myers Tobacco Co., 5" x 3", $150.00 – 200.00. Courtesy of Bob & Sherri Copeland.

Viceroy flat 50 cigarette tin by Brown & Williamson Tobacco Corp., Louisville, Kentucky, ¾" x 6½" x 4¼", $75.00 – 100.00. Courtesy of Bob & Sherri Copeland.

VIM Mixture by Gravely & Miller, Danville Virginia, marked Hasker & Marcuse, Richmond, Virginia, 1¾" x 4" x 3", $150.00 – 200.00. Courtesy of Grant Smith.

Virginia Flakes by Wm. S. Kimball & Co., Rochester, New York, 1¾" x 3¾" x 4½", $75.00 – 100.00. Courtesy of Mike & Sharon Hunt.

Wake Up paper label by Moore & Calvi, New York, 6¼" x 4¾", $600.00 – 700.00.
Courtesy of Wm. Morford Auctions.

Wascana by Wascana Cigar Factory, Kampen, Holland, 2½" x 9" x 5", $300.00 – 350.00. Courtesy of Ken & Nancy Jones.

Wascana by Wascana Cigar Factory, Kampen, Holland, ¾" x 3¾" x 3½", $150.00 – 200.00.
Courtesy of Grant Smith.

Week End vertical pocket cigarette tin by Singleton & Cole Ltd., 3" x 2½" x 1¼", $250.00 – 300.00.

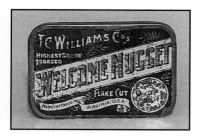

Welcome Nugget by T.C. Williams Co., Virginia, ½" x 3¼" x 2¼", $25.00 – 50.00. Courtesy of Grant Smith.

Weldon (dragon) vertical pocket by Cobb, Bates, & Yerxa Co., Boston, Massachusetts, 3½" x 3½" x 1", rare, no price available.

Westminster vertical pocket cigarette case by Westminster Tobacco Co. Ltd., London, 3" x 3" x 1¼", $50.00 – 75.00.

White Ash flat 50 cigarette tin by G.B. Van Huet, Rotterdam, Holland, ¾" x 6¼" x 4¾", $75.00 – 100.00. Courtesy of Bob & Sherri Copeland.

White House Mixture by Broomall & Wogan, Philadelphia, marked Hasker & Marcuse, 2¼" x 4½" x 3¼", $1,500.00 – 1,750.00. Courtesy of Grant Smith.

White Owl (blue) by Imperial Tobacco Co., Canada, 5¾" x 5½", $450.00 – 500.00. Courtesy of Wm. Morford Auctions.
Note: A white variation exists with much less value.

Wigwam by The Rock City Tobacco Co., marked MacDonald, 3¾" x 5" x 3½", $1,250.00 – 1,500.00. Courtesy of Grant Smith.

Willem II flat cigar tin, made in Holland, ¾" x 3¾" x 1¾", $1.00 – 25.00.

Winchester flat 50 cigarette tin by Imperial Tobacco Co. of Canada, ¾" x 5¾" x 4½", $25.00 – 50.00.
Courtesy of Bob & Sherri Copeland.

Wm. Penn vertical cigar box, 4¾" x 3" x 3", $25.00 – 50.00.

World's Standard by West, Stone & Co., Springfield, Massachusetts, 1½" x 4½" x 3¼", $150.00 – 200.00. Courtesy of Grant Smith.

Yellow Cab cigar canisters marked American Can Co. 70A, left: 5½" x 5½"; right: 5½" x 2½"; $1,750.00 – 2,000.00 ea. Courtesy of Grant Smith.

Zaphirio cigarette tin by A. Zaphiro & Co., 5¾" x 4½" x ½", $75.00 – 100.00.
Courtesy of Buffalo Bay Auction Co.

Arm & Hammer sample by Church & Dwight Co. Inc., New York, 2¼" x 2¼" x 1", $50.00 – 75.00. Courtesy of Lawson & Lin Veasey

Blue Ribbon, 3 pounds, $50.00 – 75.00. Courtesy of Buffalo Bay Auction Co.

Bob-White cardboard with tin top and bottom, 3½" x 2", $75.00 – 100.00. Courtesy of Buffalo Bay Auction Co.

Calumet by General Foods Corp., Chicago, 4¼" x 2½", $1.00 – 25.00 ea.

Calumet paper label by Calumet Baking Powder Co., Chicago, Illinois, 8" x 5½", $25.00 – 50.00. Courtesy of Tom & Mary Lou Slike.

Chef by Ocean Mills Ltd., Montreal, Canada, 5" x 3", $50.00 – 75.00. Courtesy of Alex & Marilyn Znaiden.

Cleveland's Superior paper label by Cleveland Bros., Albany, New York, 3½" x 2", $25.00 – 50.00. Courtesy of Buffalo Bay Auction Co.

Common Sense sample by Canby, Ach & Canby Co., Dayton, Ohio, 2½" x 1¾", $75.00 – 100.00. Courtesy of Richard & Ann Lehmann.

Crescent by Crescent Manufacturing Co., Seattle, Washington, $1.00 – 25.00. Courtesy of Buffalo Bay Auction Co.

Donavan's paper label from Mt. Morris, New York, 5¼" x 3", $100.00 – 150.00. Courtesy of Wm. Morford Auctions.

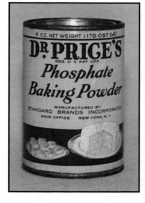

Dr. Price's paper label by Standard Brands Inc., New York, New York, 4½" x 2½", $25.00 – 50.00. Courtesy of Richard & Ann Lehmann.

Egg-O by Egg-O Baking Powder Co., Hamilton, Canada, 5" x 3", $75.00 – 100.00. Courtesy of Richard & Ann Lehmann.

Empress Canadian tin, 4½" x 3", $150.00 – 200.00. Courtesy of Wm. Morford Auctions.

Fancy-Pastry by B. Heller & Co., Chicago, Illinois, 9¾" x 7", $600.00 – 700.00. Courtesy of Alex & Marilyn Znaiden.

Fleischmann's by Fleischmann's Yeast Inc., Greenville, Texas, 9½" x 6¾", $1.00 – 25.00.

Good Luck cardboard with tin top and bottom by Southern Mfg. Co., Richmond, Virginia, 4½" x 2", $25.00 – 50.00. Courtesy of Bob & Sherri Copeland.

Jewel T by Jewel Tea Co. Inc., Barrington, Illinois, $25.00 – 50.00. Courtesy of Buffalo Bay Auction Co.

Jewel T by Jewel T Co., New York–Chicago, 5½" x 2¾", $50.00 – 75.00. Courtesy of Bob & Sherri Copeland.

KC by Jaques Mfg. Co., Chicago, Illinois, 4" x 2½", $25.00 – 50.00. Courtesy of Richard & Ann Lehmann.

Krout's cardboard with tin top and bottom by Albert Krout, $500.00 – 600.00. Courtesy of Wm. Morford Auctions.

Ladies' Friends paper label, 3½" x 2", $75.00 – 100.00. Courtesy of Buffalo Bay Auction Co.

Luxury paper label by C.F. Ware Coffee Co., Dayton, Ohio, 3¼" x 2", $100.00 – 150.00.

Manhattan cardboard with tin top & bottom by United Naval Stores Co. Inc., New York, New York, 3½" x 2", $25.00 – 50.00. Courtesy of Buffalo Bay Auction Co.

Mascot cardboard with tin top and bottom, 3½" x 2", $50.00 – 75.00. Courtesy of Buffalo Bay Auction Co.

Miss Princine paper label by Southern Mfg. Co., Richmond, Virginia, 3¾" x 3¾", $50.00 – 75.00. Courtesy of Tom & Mary Lou Slike.

Musgo cardboard with tin top and bottom by Christie-Collar Co., 5" x 2", $50.00 – 75.00. Courtesy of Buffalo Bay Auction Co.

Parke's cardboard with tin top and bottom, 4" x 2", $25.00 – 50.00. Courtesy of Buffalo Bay Auction Co.

Parrot and Monkey paper label, 3½" x 2", $75.00 – 100.00. Courtesy of Wm. Morford Auctions.

Quaker Maid paper label, 3¼" x 2¼", $25.00 – 50.00. Courtesy of Buffalo Bay Auction Co.

Rose by Integrity Mills, Toronto, Canada, marked A.C. Co. 29A, 5¼" x 3", $50.00 – 75.00.

Rough Rider paper label by The Southern Mfg. Co., Richmond, Virginia, 4" x 2", $50.00 – 75.00. Courtesy of Bob & Sherri Copeland.

Royal by Standard Brands Inc., New York, left: 4¾" x 3", $1.00 – 25.00; center: paper label, 4" x 2½", $1.00 – 25.00; right: sample, 2¾" x 2", $75.00 – 100.00.

Sea Gull paper label by The Sea Gull Co., Baltimore, Maryland, 3¼" x 2", $200.00 – 250.00. Courtesy of Wm. Morford Auctions.

Snow Flake paper label by W.F. Smith Co. Druggest & Chemist, Plainsville, Ohio, 5½" x 3¼", $100.00 – 150.00. Courtesy of Tom & Mary Lou Slike.

Snow King paper label by Snow King Baking Powder Co., 4" x 2½", $25.00 – 50.00. Courtesy of Bob & Sherri Copeland.

Snow King sample paper label by Snow King Baking Powder Co., Cincinnati, Ohio, 3" x 2", $50.00 – 75.00. Courtesy of Bob & Sherri Copeland.

Standard by Calumet Tea & Coffee Co., Chicago, Illinois, 9¾" x 7", $100.00 – 150.00. Courtesy of Alex & Marilyn Znaiden.

Staley's by A.E. Staley Mfg. Co., Baltimore, Maryland, 3½" x 2", $25.00 – 50.00.

Swan's Down by S.S. Pierce Co., marked Ginna & Co., 3" x 5" x 3", $150.00 – 200.00. Courtesy of Bob & Sherri Copeland.
Note: A paper label version exists with less value.

Vision paper label, 4¼" x 2½", $150.00 – 200.00. Courtesy of Wm. Morford Auctions.

White Cap paper label by Jas. Heekin & Co., Cincinnati, Ohio, 3½" x 2", $25.00 – 50.00. Courtesy of Bob & Sherri Copeland.

Zanol paper label by The Zanol Products Co., Cincinnati, Ohio, 5¼" x 3", $25.00 – 50.00. Courtesy of Richard & Ann Lehmann.

···❖···

COFFEE TINS

1147 by Buffalo Butter & Egg
Co., Buffalo, New York, 3½" x
5", $50.00 – 75.00. Courtesy of Buffalo
Bay Auction Co.

5-More by E.C. Conroy Coffee
Co., Kansas City, Kansas, 3½" x
5", $25.00 – 50.00. Courtesy of Buffalo
Bay Auction Co.

#730 by Consolidated Foods Inc., Chicago,
Illinois, 3½" x 5", $25.00 – 50.00. Courtesy of
Tom & Lynne Sankiewicz.

Acme by American Stores Co., Philadelphia, Pennsylvania, 4" x 5", $25.00 –
50.00. Courtesy of Bob & Sherri Copeland.

Admiration by Duncan Coffee
Co., Houston Texas, 3½" x 5",
$25.00 – 50.00. Courtesy of Buffalo Bay
Auction Co.

After Glow by Western Grocer
Mills, Marshalltown, Iowa, 8" x
6", $75.00 – 100.00. Courtesy of Buffalo
Bay Auction Co.

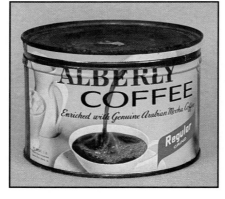

Aladdin by M.J. Branden-
stein & Co., San Francisco,
$200.00 – 250.00.

Alberly by Colonial Stores Inc.,
Havana, Georgia, 3½" x 5", $25.00 –
50.00.

Alpine by Nestlé, San
Francisco, California, 5½"
x 4¾", $75.00 – 100.00.
Courtesy of Buffalo Bay Auction Co.

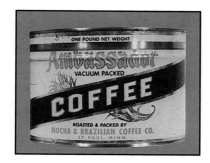

Ambassador by Mocha & Brazilian Coffee Co., St. Paul, Minnesota, 3½" x 5", $25.00 – 50.00. Courtesy of Buffalo Bay Auction Co.

American Breakfast by H.L. MacKinnon Co. Ltd, Winnipeg, aprox. 9" x 8", $25.00 – 50.00. Courtesy of Buffalo Bay Auction Co.

American Home cardboard with tin top and bottom, 6" x 4", $250.00 – 300.00. Courtesy of Buffalo Bay Auction Co.

American House by American Grocery Co., Hoboken, New Jersey, 5¾" x 4¼", $75.00 – 100.00. Courtesy of Buffalo Bay Auction Co.

American Lady by Haas Lieber Grocery Co., St. Louis, Missouri, left: 9½" x 5½", $800.00 – 900.00; center: 6" x 4¼", $1,750.00 – 2,000.00; right: 9½" x 5½", $700.00 – 800.00. Courtesy of Alex & Marilyn Znaiden.

Arabian Banquet, 6" x 4", $200.00 – 250.00. Courtesy of Buffalo Bay Auction Co.

Arco by Andresen Ryan Coffee Co., Duluth, Minnesota, 3¾" x 5", $25.00 – 50.00. Courtesy of Buffalo Bay Auction Co.

Ariel Club by C.H. Kroneberger &
Co., Baltimore, Maryland, marked
A.C. Co. 14A, 4" x 5", $200.00 –
250.00. Courtesy of Bob & Sherri Copeland.

Aunt Minerva by S & D Coffee
Co., Concord, North Carolina,
7½" x 6", $500.00 – 600.00. Cour-
tesy of Wm. Morford Auctions.

Aunt Nellie's by Harrisburg Grocery
Co., Harrisburg, Pennsylvania,
3½" x 5", $200.00 – 250.00. Courtesy
of Buffalo Bay Auction Co.

Bailey's Surpreme by Southland Coffee Co.
Inc., Richmond, Virginia, 4" x 5", $25.00 –
50.00. Courtesy of Tom & Lynne Sankiewicz.

Beard's Old Government by S.N. Beard
Sons Co., 6½" x 4½", $350.00 – 400.00.
Courtesy of Alex & Marilyn Znaiden.

Bell, The, by J.H. Bell & Co., Chicago, Illinois, hand stenciled
by Magnolia Mills, $250.00 – 300.00. Courtesy of Buffalo Bay Auction Co.

Belle Cup by Household Products Co., Evanston, Illinois, 3½" x 5", $150.00 – 200.00. Courtesy of Buffalo Bay Auction Co.

Big Value by Carolina Coffee Co., Charleston, South Carolina, marked Canco, 3¾" x 5", $25.00 – 50.00.

Bird Brand by German American Coffee Co., Omaha, Nebraska, 14" x 5", $150.00 – 200.00. Courtesy of Buffalo Bay Auction Co.

Blend 150 by Coffee Corporation of America, Chicago, Illinois, 3½" x 5", $1.00 – 25.00. Courtesy of Tom & Lynne Sankiewicz.

Blue Bird, 7" x 6½", $200.00 – 250.00. Courtesy of Buffalo Bay Auction Co.

Blue Flame, 3 pounds, 9" x 5", $200.00 – 250.00. Courtesy of Buffalo Bay Auction Co.

Blue Knot by Davies-Strauss-Stauffer Co., Easton, Pennsylvania, 4" x 5", $50.00 – 75.00. Courtesy of Buffalo Bay Auction Co.

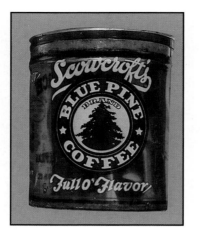

Blue Pine by Scowcroft's, 5¾" x 4¼", $75.00 – 100.00. Courtesy of Buffalo Bay Auction Co.

Blue Ribbon by The Ulry-Talbert Co., Grand Island, Nebraska, 3½" x 5", $25.00 – 50.00. Courtesy of Buffalo Bay Auction Co.

Boardman's by Wm. Boardman & Sons Co., Hartford, Connecticut, marked A.C. Co. 14A, 3½" x 5", $200.00 – 250.00.

Breakfast Call by The Independent Coffee & Spice Co., Denver, Colorado, 9¼" x 6", $75.00 – 100.00. Courtesy of Bob & Sherri Copeland.

Bridal Brand by Thomas Roberts & Co., Philadelphia, Pennsylvania, 6" x 4¾" x 3½", $700.00 – 800.00. Courtesy of Alex & Marilyn Znaiden.

Bright and Early by Duncan
Coffee Co., Houston, Texas,
3½" x 5", $150.00 – 200.00.
Courtesy of Buffalo Bay Auction Co.

Bright and Early by Duncan Coffee Co.,
Houston, Texas, 8¼" x 9½", $200.00 –
250.00. Courtesy of Lawson & Lin Veasey.

Brite-Mawnin by Behring-Stahl
Coffee Co., 5¾" x 4¼", $100.00 –
150.00. Courtesy of Buffalo Bay Auction Co.

Brown Berry by The Wm. Boardman & Sons Co., Division of
Arnold & Aborn Inc., New York,
New York, 3½" x 5", $50.00 –
75.00. Courtesy of Buffalo Bay Auction Co.

Brown Gold made in Palisades
Park, New Jersey, 3½" x 5", $50.00
– 75.00. Courtesy of Buffalo Bay Auction Co.

Brunswick by Eldridge Baker
Co., Boston, Massachusetts, 6"
x 4", $75.00 – 100.00. Courtesy of
Buffalo Bay Auction Co.

Bungalo by National Coffee Co., Greenville,
South Carolina & Charlotte, North Carolina, left:
7¼" x 6¼", $250.00 – 300.00; right: 5½" x 4¼",
$500.00 – 600.00. Courtesy of Alex & Marilyn Znaiden.

Burma Brand made in Boston, Massachusetts, 3½" x 5", $50.00 – 75.00. Courtesy of Buffalo Bay Auction Co.

Café Blue Mountain, Canadian, 3½" x 5", $50.00 – 75.00. Courtesy of Buffalo Bay Auction Co.

Café Bustelo by Bustelo Coffee Roasting Co., Bronx, New York, marked Canco, 3½" x 5", $50.00 – 75.00.

Caliph by Interstate Tea Co., Brooklyn, New York, $50.00 – 75.00. Courtesy of Buffalo Bay Auction Co.

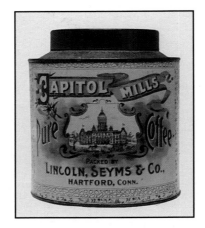

Capitol Mills by Lincoln, Seyms & Co., Hartford, Connecticut, 5½" x 4¾", $500.00 – 600.00. Courtesy of Wm. Morford Auctions.

Carnation by Closset & Devers, Portland & Seattle, 6" x 4¼", $250.00 – 300.00. Courtesy of Alex & Marilyn Znaiden.

Carnation Brand by Hulman Coffee Co., Terre Haute, Indiana, 8" x 8", $150.00 – 200.00. Courtesy of Mike & Sharon Hunt.

Carolina Belle paper label by Levering Coffee Co., Baltimore, Maryland, 6" x 4¼", $25.00 – 50.00.

Castle Blend by Castle Blend Tea Co., Montreal, Canada, 5" x 4½", $250.00 – 300.00. Courtesy of Grant Smith.

Caswell Blend by Geo. W. Caswell Co., San Francisco, California, 8¾" x 5¼", $75.00 – 100.00. Courtesy of Buffalo Bay Auction Co.

Chateau Frontenac by Kearney Bros. Ltd., Montreal & New York, 6½" x 4", $150.00 – 200.00. Courtesy of Grant Smith.

Chimes, The, paper label, 5¾" x 4¼", $100.00 – 150.00. Courtesy of Buffalo Bay Auction Co.

Clark's by Clark & Host Co., Milwaukee, Wisconsin, 5¾" x 4½", $50.00 – 75.00. Courtesy of Bob & Correna Anderson.

Clark's Favorite by Clark & Host Co., Milwaukee, Wisconsin, 3¾" x 5", $50.00 – 75.00. Courtesy of Buffalo Bay Auction Co.

Club House, 3¾" x 5", $50.00 – 75.00. Courtesy of Buffalo Bay Auction Co.

Coffee House by Bacon Stickney & Co. Inc., Albany, New York, 3¾" x 5", $200.00 – 250.00. Courtesy of Buffalo Bay Auction Co.

College Town by H.G. Distributing Co., New Brunswick, New Jersey, 6¼" x 4", $900.00 – 1,000.00. Courtesy of Alex & Marilyn Znaiden.

Colonial by Thomas Coffee Co., York, Pennsylvania, marked A.C. Co. 10A, 6" x 4¼", $200.00 – 250.00. Courtesy of Grant Smith.

Columbia by W.F. McLaughlin & Co., Chicago, Illinois, 4" x 5", $50.00 – 75.00. Courtesy of Buffalo Bay Auction Co.

Commonwealth paper label by J.F. Nickerson Co. Boston, Massachusetts, 5½" x 4½", $100.00 – 150.00. Courtesy of Buffalo Bay Auction Co.

Comrade by J.A. Folger & Co., San Francisco, California, 3½" x 5", $100.00 – 150.00. Courtesy of Buffalo Bay Auction Co.

Constitution by E.T. Smith Co., Worcester, Massachusetts, 3½" x 5", no price available. Courtesy of Bob & Correna Anderson.

Convention Hall by Ridenour-Baker Grocery Co., Kansas City, Missouri, 6¼" x 4¼", $200.00 – 250.00. Courtesy of Grant Smith.

Court House by C.F. Smith Stores, Detroit, Michigan, 3½" x 5", $200.00 – 250.00. Courtesy of Buffalo Bay Auction Co.

Crawford's Best by James Crawford & Co., Philadelphia, Pennsylvania, 3½" x 5", $75.00 – 100.00. Courtesy of Buffalo Bay Auction Co.

CW Brand by The Widlar Co., Cleveland, Ohio, 5¾" x 4¼", $25.00 – 50.00.

D.C. & H. by Driscol, Church & Hall Inc., Bedford, Massachusetts, marked Passaic Metalware Co., Passaic, New Jersey, 6" x 4", $450.00 – 500.00. Courtesy of Alex & Marilyn Znaiden.

Dauntless paper label by Hulman & Co., Terre Haute, Indiana, 6" x 4", $100.00 – 150.00. Courtesy of Buffalo Bay Auction Co.

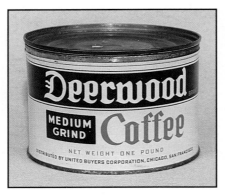

Deerwood by United Buyers Corp., Chicago & San Francisco, 3½" x 5", $1.00 – 25.00. Courtesy of Bob & Sherri Copeland.

Deerwood by Copps Coffee Co., Stevens Point, Wisconsin, 3¾" x 5", $250.00 – 300.00. Courtesy of Buffalo Bay Auction Co.

*Defianc*e by Jobbers Service Inc., Coldwater, Michigan, 4" x 5", $75.00 – 100.00.

DeLuxe, 3 pound, 8¾" x 6¼", $50.00 – 75.00. Courtesy of Buffalo Bay Auction Co.

Dependon made in Minneapolis, MN, 3½" x 5", $100.00 – 150.00. Courtesy of Buffalo Bay Auction Co.

Derby by Meyer-Schmid Grocer Co., St Louis, 7" x 5" x 5", $300.00 – 350.00. Courtesy of Ken & Nancy Jones.

Dilworth's Golden Urn by Dilworth Co., Pittsburg, Pennsylvania, marked A.C. Co. 27A, 4" x 5", $150.00 – 200.00. Courtesy of Alex & Marilyn Znaiden.

Dinner Party by Black Hawk Coffee & Spice Co., Waterloo, Iowa, 10" x 7", $100.00 – 150.00. Courtesy of Buffalo Bay Auction Co.

Donald Duck sample by Goyer Coffee Co., Greenville, Mississippi, 2¼" x 3", $500.00 – 600.00. Courtesy of Lawson & Lin Veasey.

Dutch Girl by The Eureka Coffee Co., Buffalo, New York, 6½" x 4¼" x 3", $100.00 – 150.00. Courtesy of Wm. Morford Auctions.

Eatmore Brand, 3¾" x 5", $75.00 – 100.00. Courtesy of Buffalo Bay Auction Co.

E-Jay by The E.J. Evans Co., Van Wert, Ohio, 3½" x 5", $1.00 – 25.00. Courtesy of Tom & Lynne Sankiewicz.

Empress by Stone Ordean Wells Co., Duluth, Minnesota, 3¾" x 5", $100.00 – 150.00. Courtesy of Buffalo Bay Auction Co.

Elephant Brand by Jewett & Sherman Co., Milwaukee, 7¾" x 7½", $500.00 – 600.00. Courtesy of Alex & Marilyn Znaiden.

Engelhard's (Grandma's Cup) by A. Engelhard & Sons Co., Louisville, Kentucky, 8¼" x 6½", $150.00 – 200.00. Courtesy of Alex & Marilyn Znaiden.

Evans American Jack by David G. Evans Coffee Co., St. Louis, 8" x 6¾", $400.00 – 450.00. Courtesy of Wm. Morford Auctions.

Fairy Dell by Oakford & Fahnestock, Peoria, Illinois, 8" x 7½", $100.00 – 150.00. Courtesy of Ken & Nancy Jones.

Feast Brand by The Ulry-Talbert Co., Grand Island, Nebraska, $75.00 – 100.00. Courtesy of Buffalo Bay Auction Co.

Federal Club paper label by Euclid Coffee Co., Cleveland, Ohio, 5½" x 4¼", $250.00 – 300.00. Courtesy of Wm. Morford Auctions.

Feilbach's by The Feilbach Co., Toledo, Ohio, 3½" x 5", $25.00 – 50.00. Courtesy of Tom & Lynne Sankiewicz.

Fireside by Fireside Coffee Co., Nashville, Tennessee, 3¾" x 5", $75.00 – 100.00. Courtesy of Buffalo Bay Auction Co.

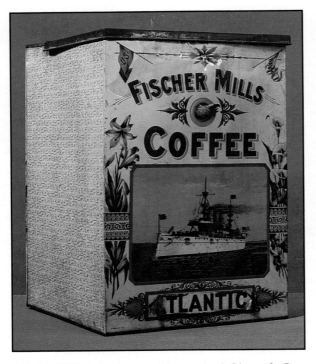

Fischer Mills Atlantic store bin marked Ginna & Co., 19¾" x 13" x 13½", $2,500.00 – 3,000.00. Courtesy of Alex & Marilyn Znaiden.

Flaroma by Grand Union Tea Co., Brooklyn, New York, 6" x 4", $25.00 – 50.00. Courtesy of Buffalo Bay Auction Co.

Flav-O-Rich by Super Value Stores Inc., Hopkins, Minnesota, 3½" x 5", $1.00 – 25.00. Courtesy of Tom & Lynne Sankiewicz.

Foley's by Foley Grocery Co., St. Paul, Minnesota, 4" x 5", $250.00 – 300.00. Courtesy of Buffalo Bay Auction Co.

Food Club by Topco Assn. Inc., Skokie & Chicago, Illinois, 3½" x 5", $1.00 – 25.00. Courtesy of Tom & Lynne Sankiewicz.

Forbes Golden Cup by Jas. H. Forbes Tea & Coffee Co., St. Louis, Missouri, 9" x 6", $150.00 – 200.00. Courtesy of Buffalo Bay Auction Co.

Fox Point by Tindall, Kolbe, & McDowell Co., Milwaukee, Wisconsin, 4" x 5", $50.00 – 75.00. Courtesy of Buffalo Bay Auction Co.

Fox by Fox Grocery Co., Charleroi & Uniontown, Pennsylvania, marked Passaic Metalware Co., Passaic, New Jersey, 6" x 4", $200.00 – 250.00.

Franco-American by Young & Griffin Coffee Co. Inc., New York, New York, 6" x 4¼" x 3", $25.00 – 50.00. Courtesy of Tom & Mary Lou Slike.

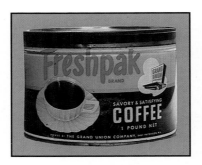

French Opera by American Coffee Co., New Orleans, 7¼" x 6", $100.00 – 150.00. Courtesy of Wm. Morford Auctions.

Freshpak Brand by The Grand Union Co., East Patterson, New Jersey, 3½" x 5", $50.00 – 75.00. Courtesy of Buffalo Bay Auction Co.

Gamble's by Gamble Stores, 3½" x 5", $25.00 – 50.00. Courtesy of Buffalo Bay Auction Co.

Gernold paper label by Baraboo Wholesale Co., Baraboo, Wisconsin, 3½" x 9¾", $25.00 – 50.00. Courtesy of Mike & Sharon Hunt.

Glendora by Glendora Products Co., Warren, Pennsylvania, 4" x 5", $25.00 – 50.00. Courtesy of Bob & Sherri Copeland.

Goddard's (Dessert Brand) by The Goddard Grocer Co., St. Louis, Missouri, 7" x 5" x 5", $250.00 – 300.00. Courtesy of Ken & Nancy Jones.

Gold Plume by Ft. Smith Coffee Co., Ft. Smith, Arkansas, 4" x 5¼", $100.00 – 150.00. Courtesy of Alex & Marilyn Znaiden.

Gold Shield by Scwabacker Bros. & Co., Seattle, Washington, 3½" x 5", $25.00 – 50.00. Courtesy of Buffalo Bay Auction Co.

Golden Days by Wm. Schotten & Co., St. Louis, 6" x 6" x 3", $150.00 – 200.00. Courtesy of Buffalo Bay Auction Co.

Golden Hour made in New York, 3½" x 5", $25.00 – 50.00. Courtesy of Buffalo Bay Auction Co.

Golden Sun paper label by Woolson Spice Co., Toledo, Ohio, $100.00 – 150.00. Courtesy of Buffalo Bay Auction Co.

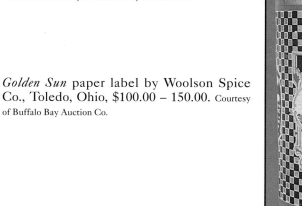

Golden Pheasant marked F & Co. Registered, 6¼" x 3¾", no price available. Courtesy of Grant Smith.

Golden Wedding by Certified Brands Inc., Kansas City, Missouri, 3½" x 5", $25.00 – 50.00. Courtesy of Tom & Lynne Sankiewicz.

Golden West by Closset & Devers, Portland, Oregon, 6¾" x 6", $100.00 – 150.00. Courtesy of Wm. Morford Auctions.

Goodhonest by Lewis DeGroff & Son, New York, 5½" x 4¼", $300.00 – 350.00. Courtesy of Wm. Morford Auctions.

Grosse Pointe by Grosse Pointe Quality Food Co., Detroit, Michigan, 3½" x 5", $1.00 – 25.00 ea. Courtesy of Bob & Sherri Copeland.

Halco, 4 pounds, 9" x 7½", $100.00 – 150.00. Courtesy of Buffalo Bay Auction Co.

Hales Leader by Hale-Halsell Co., McAlester, Oklahoma, 3½" x 5", $75.00 – 100.00. Courtesy of Buffalo Bay Auction Co.

Hansen by John Hansen & Son, Oakland, Maryland, 5¾" x 4¼", $25.00 – 50.00. Courtesy of Buffalo Bay Auction Co.

Happy Hour sample by Cambell Holton & Co., Bloomington, Illinois, 2½" x 2", $150.00 – 200.00. Courtesy of Wm. Morford Auctions.

Happy Hour by General Coffee Co., St. Louis, Missouri, 3½" x 5", $25.00 – 50.00. Courtesy of Buffalo Bay Auction Co.

Harmony Blend cardboard with tin top and bottom by Henry Siegel, New York, 11" x 7" x 5¼", $400.00 – 450.00. Courtesy of Grant Smith.

Hart's by Jas. E. Hart, Cincinnati, Ohio, marked Heedin Can Co., 6" x 4¼", $100.00 – 150.00. Courtesy of Bob & Sherri Copeland.

Harvest Queen, 3½" x 5", $50.00 – 75.00. Courtesy of Buffalo Bay Auction Co.

Health Brand by Lewis DeGroff & Son, New York, 6" x 4¼", $200.00 – 250.00. Courtesy of Alex & Marilyn Znaiden.

Heidi made in Washington, D.C., 3¾" x 5", $300.00 – 350.00. Courtesy of Buffalo Bay Auction Co.

Heinz by N.J. Heinz & Co.,
Pittsburgh, Pennsylvania, 4" x
5", $50.00 – 75.00. Courtesy of Buffalo
Bay Auction Co.

HGF Brand by The H.D. Lee Co.
Inc., Kansas City, Missouri, and
Salina, Kansas, 4" x 5", $75.00 –
100.00. Courtesy of Buffalo Bay Auction Co.

Hi-Ho by American Store Co.,
Philadelphia, Pennsylvania, 3½" x
5", $25.00 – 50.00. Courtesy of Buffalo
Bay Auction Co.

Holland's Far-East by Holland's
Far East Tea, Coffee & Cocoa
Co., Boston, Massachusetts, 4"
x 5", $50.00 – 75.00. Courtesy of
Buffalo Bay Auction CO.

Hollywood Brand made in Seattle,
Washington, 3½" x 5", $25.00 –
50.00. Courtesy of Buffalo Bay Auction Co.

Home Pride by Hal Omar Baking Co.,
Cleveland, Ohio, 3½" x 5", $1.00 – 25.00.
Courtesy of Tom & Lynne Sankiewicz.

House of Lords by Martin Gillet
& Co. Inc., Baltimore, Mary-
land, 3½" x 5", $25.00 – 50.00.
Courtesy of Buffalo Bay Auction Co.

Howell's Best by Warfield Pratt,
Howell Co., Cedar Rapids, Iowa,
Washington, 6¼" x 4¼" x 3",
$200.00 – 250.00. Courtesy of Ken &
Nancy Jones.

Hub Brand by Hub Grocer
Co., Jackson, Michigan, 4¼" x
5¼", $200.00 – 250.00. Courtesy
of Wm. Morford Auctions.

Hy-Klas by Beaty Grocery Co. Inc., St. Joseph, Missouri, 3¾" x 5", $25.00 – 50.00. Courtesy of Buffalo Bay Auction Co.

Hygeia by Browning & Baines Inc., Washington, D.C., marked C.C. Co., 3½" x 5", $50.00 – 75.00.

IGA by Independent Grocers Alliance Distributing Co., Chicago, Illinois, 4" x 5", $50.00 – 75.00.

Iris by Smart & Final Iris Co., Los Angeles, California, 3½" x 5", $50.00 – 75.00. Courtesy of Buffalo Bay Auction Co.

Ja-San-Mo by Meyer Bros. Coffee & Spice Co., St Louis, Missouri, marked Columbia Can Co., 7¼" x 5" x 5", $450.00 – 500.00. Courtesy of Alex & Marilyn Znaiden.

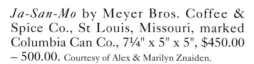

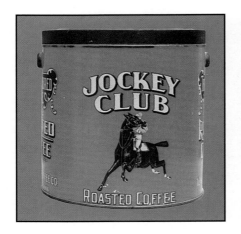

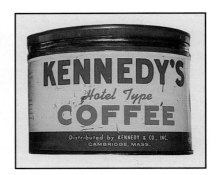

Kennedy's by Kennedy & Co. Inc., Cambridge, Massachusetts, 3½" x 5", $25.00 – 50.00. Courtesy of Buffalo Bay Auction Co.

Jockey Club, 8" x 7½", $600.00 – 700.00. Courtesy of Wm. Morford Auctions.

Kaffee Hag by The Kaffee Hag Corp., 6" x 4¼", $25.00 – 50.00. Courtesy of Bob & Sherri Copeland.

Kimbell's by Kimbell's Coffee & Tea Corp., Fort Worth, Texas, 3½" x 5", $1.00 – 25.00. Courtesy of Tom & Lynne Sankiewicz.

King Mogul by Consumers Mill Product Co., Kansas City, Missouri, 8" x 6", $100.00 – 150.00. Courtesy of Buffalo Bay Auction Co.

King Othon paper label, 6" x 3½", $75.00 – 100.00. Courtesy of Buffalo Bay Auction Co.

Kohl's Superfine by N. Kohl Grocer Co., Quincy, Illinois, 6" x 4", $350.00 – 400.00. Courtesy of Ken & Nancy Jones.

Leggett's Champion Java by Francis H. Leggett & Co., marked Ginna & Co., New York, 9½" x 5" x 5", $300.00 – 350.00. Courtesy of Alex & Marilyn Znaiden.

Life by James E. Hart, Cincinnati, Ohio, 3½" x 5", $50.00 – 75.00. Courtesy of Buffalo Bay Auction Co.

Lindy Lou by Watkins Coffee Co., Charlotte, North Carolina, 7½" x 7½", $400.00 – 450.00.

Little Elf by G.E. Bursley & Co., Fort Wayne & Elkhart, Indiana, 5¾" x 4¼", $350.00 – 400.00. Courtesy of Alex & Marilyn Znaiden.

Lucky Cup made in Brooklyn, New York, 4" x 5", $150.00 – 200.00. Courtesy of Buffalo Bay Auction Co.

Log Cabin by Shafer Stores, Altoona, Pennsylvania, 4" x 5", $1,000.00 – 1,250.00. Courtesy of Wm. Morford Auctions.

Lucky Jack by J.W. Jaeger, Columbus, Ohio, 4" x 5", $100.00 – 150.00. Courtesy of Bob & Sherri Copeland.

Magnolia by Magnolia Coffee Co., Houston, Texas, 3½" x 5", $150.00 – 200.00. Courtesy of Buffalo Bay Auction Co.

Macy's Red Star by R.H. Macy & Co. Inc., New York, 6" x 4¼", $25.00 – 50.00. Courtesy of Bob & Sherri Copeland.

Mammy's by C.D. Kenny Co., Buffalo, New York, 10½" x 6", $300.00. – 350.00.

Market Basket by Market Basket, Los Angeles, California, 3½" x 5", $25.00 – 50.00. Courtesy of Buffalo Bay Auction Co.

Marsh by Marsh Supermarkets, Inc., Yorktown, Indiana, 3½" x 5", $50.00 – 75.00. Courtesy of Buffalo Bay Auction Co.

Maryland Club sample by The Coca Cola Co. Foods Division, Houston, Texas, 2¼" x 2¼", $25.00 – 50.00.

Matchless by Webster Thomas Co., Boston, Massachusetts, 6" x 4", $100.00 – 150.00. Courtesy of Ken & Nancy Jones.

Maxwell House vendo by General Foods Corp., White Plains, New York, 2½" x 3¼", $25.00 – 50.00.

May-Day by E.B. Millar Coffee Co., Chicago & Denver, 4" x 5", $50.00 – 75.00. Courtesy of Buffalo Bay Auction Co.

McLain's by The McLain Grocery Co., Massillon, Ohio, 3½" x 5", $25.00 – 50.00.

Mellocup made in Chicago, Illinois, 3¾" x 5", $150.00 – 200.00. Courtesy of Buffalo Bay Auction Co.

Metacomet by Allen, Slade & Co., marked Ginna & Co., New York, 5" x 4¼", $800.00 – 900.00. Courtesy of Alex & Marilyn Znaiden.

Milcan by Closset & Devers, Portland and Seattle, 11" x 7¼", $200.00 – 250.00. Courtesy of Wm. Morford Auctions.

Milliken Fancy store bin by WE-CR Milliken, Portland, Maine, 22" x 13" x 13", $250.00 – 300.00. Courtesy of Alex & Marilyn Znaiden.

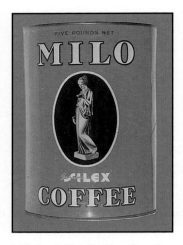

Milo by Milo Coffee Co., San Francisco, California, 9½" x 7", $100.00 – 150.00. Courtesy of Buffalo Bay Auction Co.

Minuet by Sanitary Food Manufacturing Co., New York, New York, 3½" x 5", $100.00 – 150.00. Courtesy of Buffalo Bay Auction Co.

Mocha and Java paper label by S.S. Pierce Co., Boston, Massachusetts, 6" x 4", $75.00 – 100.00. Courtesy of Buffalo Bay Auction Co.

Montauk by Keys, Corsa & Holley, New York, 6½" x 4¼", $600.00 – 700.00. Courtesy of Alex & Marilyn Znaiden.

Monticello by Pender Grocery Co., Norfolk, Virginia, 3¾" x 5", $150.00 – 200.00. Courtesy of Buffalo Bay Auction Co.

Moon Rose by Hubbard Grocery Co., Charleston, West Virginia, 3½" x 5", $300.00 – 350.00. Courtesy of Alex & Marilyn Znaiden.

Morey Mills from Denver, Colorado, marked Norton Bros., 6¾" x 6" x 3¾", $150.00 – 200.00. Courtesy of Wm. Morford Auctions.

Morning Glow by R.L. Gerhart & Co., Lancaster, Pennsylvania, 4" x 5". $100.00 – 150.00. Courtesy of Buffalo Bay Auction Co.

Morning Star made in Seattle, Washington, 3½" x 5", $50.00 – 75.00. Courtesy of Buffalo Bay Auction Co.

Morning Treat by Morning Treat Coffee Co., Baton Rouge, Louisiana, 4" x 5", $50.00 – 75.00. Courtesy of Buffalo Bay Auction Co.

Morton House by Lee & Cady, Successors to Worden Grocer Co., Michigan, 6" x 4", $50.00 – 75.00. Courtesy of Buffalo Bay Auction Co.

Motta Espresso by Motta Inc., 3½" x 5", $25.00 – 50.00. Courtesy of Buffalo Bay Auction Co.

Mount Cross by J.S. Brown Mercantile Co., Denver, Colorado, 4" x 5", $75.00 – 100.00.

Mount Cross by J.S. Brown Mercantile, Co., Denver, Colorado, 9" x 5¾", $200.00 – 250.00. Courtesy of Buffalo Bay Auction Co.

Nathor's Best made in New York, New York, 3½" x 5", $50.00 – 75.00. Courtesy of Buffalo Bay Auction Co.

Nectar Brand by St. Louis Coffee & Spice Mills, marked Columbia Can Co., 3¾" x 10", $200.00 – 250.00. Courtesy of Mike & Sharon Hunt.

Newmark's, 2 pounds, $150.00 – 200.00. Courtesy of Wm. Morford Auctions.

New Deal made in Baltimore, Maryland, 4" x 5", $25.00 – 50.00. Courtesy of Buffalo Bay Auction Co.

Rosy Morn paper label, 6" x 4", $75.00 – 100.00. Courtesy of Buffalo Bay Auction Co.

Royal Arms by Hill Bros. Inc., Miami, Florida, 3¾" x 5", $25.00 – 50.00. Courtesy of Tom & Lynne Sankiewicz.

Royal Star by McMahan & Leib Co., marked Anderson & Marion, Indiana, 4" x 5", $75.00 – 100.00. Courtesy of Buffalo Bay Auction Co.

S and W by S and W Fine Foods Inc., San Francisco, California, 3½" x 5", $25.00 – 50.00. Courtesy of Bob & Sherri Copeland.

Royal Breakfast made in Philadelphia, Pennsylvania, $100.00 – 150.00. Courtesy of Buffalo Bay Auction Co.

S and W by S and W Fine Foods Inc., San Francisco, California, $1.00 – 25.00.

Sanico by Sanitary Grocery Co. Inc., Washington, D.C., 4" x 5", $75.00 – 100.00. Courtesy of Buffalo Bay Auction Co.

Schotten's by Wm. Schotten & Co., St. Louis, marked Ginna & Co., 11" x 7" x 7", $600.00 – 700.00. Courtesy of Wm. Morford Auctions.

Seminole paper label by Denison & Co., Chicago, Illinois, 5½" x 4¼", $450.00 – 500.00. Courtesy of Wm. Morford Auctions.

Serv-Us, 6" x 4", $75.00 – 100.00. Courtesy of Buffalo Bay Auction Co.

Scull's Sterling by Wm. S. Scull Co., Camden, New Jersey, 22" x 19¼" x 13½", $700.00 – 800.00. Courtesy of Alex & Marilyn Znaiden.

Seven Day made in New York, 4" x 5", $50.00 – 75.00. Courtesy of Buffalo Bay Auction Co.

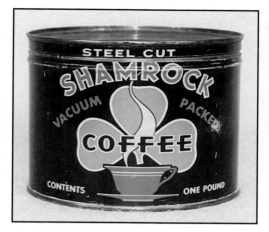

Shamrock by U.C.O. Food Corp., Newark, New Jersey, marked A.C. Co. 10A, 4" x 5", $150.00 – 200.00. Courtesy of Alex & Marilyn Znaiden.

Show Boat made in New York, New York, 3¾" x 4", $150.00 – 200.00. Courtesy of Buffalo Bay Auction Co.

Sidax made in New York, New York, 3½" x 5", $50.00 – 75.00. Courtesy of Buffalo Bay Auction Co.

Silver Moon paper label by Oliver-Finnie Co., Memphis, Tennessee, 5½" x 4¼", $450.00 – 500.00. Courtesy of Wm. Morford Auctions.

Silvercup made in Brooklyn, New York, 3¾" x 5", $100.00 – 150.00. Courtesy of Buffalo Bay Auction Co.

Southern Girl by Diamond Coffee Mills Inc., Shreveport, Louisiana, 6" x 4¼", $300.00 – 350.00. Courtesy of Alex & Marilyn Znaiden.

Splendora by Granger Co., Buffalo, New York, 5¾" x 4½", $1,250.00 – 1,500.00. Courtesy of Alex & Marilyn Znaiden.

State House paper label by Black Hawk Coffee & Spice Co., Waterloo, Iowa, 5¾" x 4¼", $350.00 – 400.00. Courtesy of Wm. Morford Auctions.

Spring Hill paper label by Berdan & Co., Toledo, Ohio, 5¼" x 4¼", $25.00 – 50.00. Courtesy of Bob & Sherri Copeland.

Stewart's by Stewart & Ashby Coffee Co., Chicago, Illinois, 3½" x 5", $25.00 – 50.00 ea. Courtesy of Bob & Sherri Copeland.

Steer Brand by Roth-Homeyer Coffee Co., St. Louis, Missouri, 6¼" x 4¼", $250.00 – 300.00. Courtesy of Grant Smith.

Stop & Shop by Stop & Shop, Boston, Massachusetts, 3½" x 5", $25.00 – 50.00. Courtesy of Buffalo Bay Auction Co.

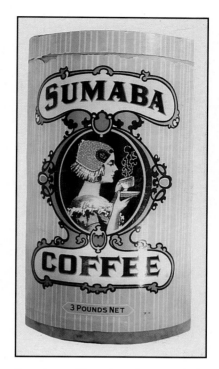

Sunflower by Dolan Mercantile Co., Atchison, Kansas, 3¾" x 5¼", $1,000.00 – 1,250.00. Courtesy of Wm. Morford Auctions.

Sundown paper label, 6" x 4", $75.00 – 100.00. Courtesy of Buffalo Bay Auction Co.

Sumaba cardboard canister made in Milwuakee, Wisconsin, 9" x 5¾", $75.00 – 100.00. Courtesy of Buffalo Bay Auction Co.

Super Value by Wm. S. Scull Co., marked Canco 3½" x 5", $25.00 – 50.00.

Sure Value by Wm. S. Scull Co Inc., Camden, New Jersey, 3½" x 5", $25.00 – 50.00. Courtesy of David Morris.

Swallow by Swallow Coffee Mills Co., Chicago, Illinois, marked A.C. Co. 70A, 5¾" x 4¼", $500.00 – 600.00. Courtesy of Grant Smith.

Symons' Best by Symons Bros. & Co. Dist., Saginaw, Michigan, 3½" x 5", $25.00 – 50.00. Courtesy of Bob & Sherri Copeland.

Tavern by Closset & Devers, Portland & Seattle, Washington, 6" x 4¼", $1,750.00 – 2,000.00. Courtesy of Grant Smith.

Thalhimers Fountain by Thalhimer's Fine Foods, Richmond, Virginia, 3½" x 5", $50.00 – 75.00. Courtesy of Buffalo Bay Auction Co.

Trexler Park made in Allentown, Pennsylvania, 3½" x 5", $75.00 – 100.00. Courtesy of Buffalo Bay Auction Co.

Trophy by Blodgett-Beckley Co., Toledo & Kansas City, 4" x 5¼", $25.00 – 50.00. Courtesy of Tom & Lynne Sankiewicz.

Trumpet, Petring's, by H-P Coffee Co., St. Louis, Missouri, 6" x 4¼", $100.00 – 150.00. Courtesy of Buffalo Bay Auction Co.

Tudor paper label by Alexander H. Bill & Co., 5½" x 4½", $100.00 – 150.00. Courtesy of Buffalo Bay Auction Co.

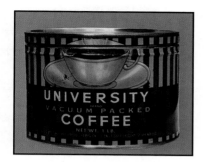

University by Fisher Grocery Co., Champaign & Springfield, Illinois, 4" x 5", $200.00 – 250.00. Courtesy of Buffalo Bay Auction Co.

Union Star paper label, 6" x 4¼", $600.00 – 700.00. Courtesy of Wm. Morford Auctions.

Twickenham by The Huntsville Coffee Co. Inc., Huntsville, Alabama, 6" x 4¼", $600.00 – 700.00. Courtesy of Alex & Marilyn Znaiden.

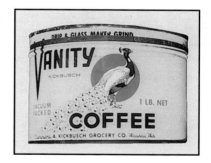

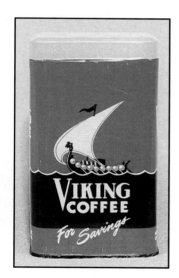

Vanity by A. Kickbusch Grocery Co., Wausau, Wisconsin, 3½" x 5", $150.00 – 200.00. Courtesy of Buffalo Bay Auction Co.

Velvet by W.H. Malkin Co., Vancouver, 9" x 8", $200.00 – 250.00. Courtesy of Wm. Morford Auctions.

Viking bank by National Retailer Owned Grocers Inc., Chicago, Illinois, 4" x 3¼" x 1¾", $1.00 – 25.00. Courtesy of Tom & Lynne Sankiewicz.

Webb by Thomas J. Webb Co., Chicago, Illinois, 3½" x 5", $1.00 – 25.00. Courtesy of Bob & Sherri Copeland.

West Point by General Tobacco & Grocery Co., Detroit, Michigan, 4" x 5", $75.00 – 100.00. Courtesy of Tom & Lynne Sankiewicz.

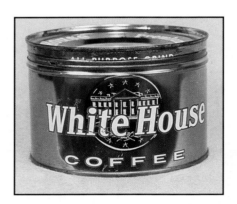

White House by Dwinell Wright Co. Inc., New York, 3½" x 5", $100.00 – 150.00. Courtesy of Bob & Sherri Copeland.

White Lilac by Consolidated Tea Co. Inc., New York, 3¾" x 5", $150.00 – 200.00. Courtesy of Alex & Marilyn Znaiden.

White Star by The Crocker Sprague Co., Dunkirk, New York, 6" x 4¼", $100.00 – 150.00. Courtesy of Buffalo Bay Auction Co.

Wilco by Williams Bros. Co., Wilkes-Barre, Pennsylvania, 6" x 4", $250.00 – 300.00. Courtesy of Alex & Marilyn Znaiden.

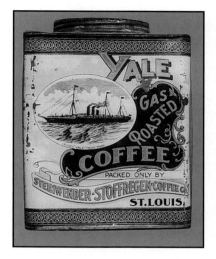

Yale by Steinwender-Stoffregen Coffee Co., St. Louis, Missouri, 8" x 5" x 5", $200.00 – 250.00. Courtesy of Buffalo Bay Auction Co.

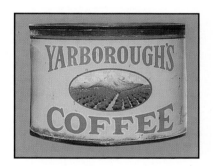

Yarborough's made in Corpus Christi, Texas, 3½" x 5", $75.00 – 100.00. Courtesy of Buffalo Bay Auction Co.

Zodiac paper label by Foltz Tea & Coffee Co., New Orleans, 5½" x 4", $75.00 – 100.00. Courtesy of Bob & Sherri Copeland.

Allen's Toffee by C.S. Allen Corp., New York, 9½" x 8¾" x 5", $50.00 – 75.00.

4 MK by Mueller-Keller Candy Co., St. Joseph, Missouri, 10" x 5¼", $25.00 – 50.00. Courtesy of Schimpff's Confectionary.

Beich's Cupid Cordials by Paul F. Beich & Co., Chicago, ½" x 1½", $1.00 – 25.00. Courtesy of Schimpff's Confectionary.

Badger Brand by Badger Candy Co., Milwaukee, marked Continental Can Co., 14" x 10", $50.00 – 75.00. Courtesy of Schimpff's Confectionary.

Brach's by E.J. Brach & Sons, Chicago, 7½" x 12½", $75.00 – 100.00. Courtesy of Schimpff's Confectionary.

Bishop's Candies by Bishop & Co., marked A.C. Co. 70A, 7½" x 5" x 5", $50.00 – 75.00. Courtesy of Schimpff's Confectionary.

Brown Betty by Hagley Candy Co., Chicago, Illinois, 1½" x 5", $1.00 – 25.00.

Bunte Opera Twist by Bunte Bros., Chicago, Illinois, marked Continental Can Co., 7" x 5½", $100.00 – 150.00. Courtesy of Schimpff's Confectionary.

Cardinet's by Cardinet Candy Co., Oakland, California, 7" x 6¼", $25.00 – 50.00. Courtesy of Schimpff's Confectionary.

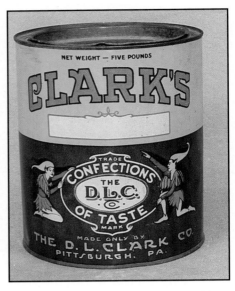

Charlie Younger's Mints marked Kirkland, Washington, A.C. Co. 92A, 4¼" x 4", $1.00 – 25.00. Courtesy of Schimpff's Confectionary.

Chop Suey by E.F. Kemp, Boston, Massachusetts, ca. 1932, 6¾" x 3", $25.00 – 50.00. Courtesy of Schimpff's Confectionary.

Clark's by The D.L. Clark Co., Pittsburgh, Pennsylvania, 7¼" x 6", $75.00 – 100.00. Courtesy of Schimpff's Confectionary.

Cummings by Cummings Corp., Philadelphia, Pennsylvania, 3¾" x 3½", $1.00 – 25.00. Courtesy of Schimpff's Confectionary.

DeMet's Century of Progress by De Mets Inc., Chicago, promotional tin for 1934 World's Fair, $50.00 – 75.00. Courtesy of Schimpff's Confectionary.

Elmer's Pecan Pralines by Elmer Candy Co., New Orleans, Louisiana, 3½" x 5", $1.00 – 25.00.
Courtesy of Bob & Sherri Copeland.

Dixie Queen by Huggins Candy Co., Nashville, Tennessee, 4¼" x 6", $1.00 – 25.00. Courtesy of Schimpff's Confectionary.

Edgar P. Lewis hard candy marked Boston, $1.00 – 25.00.
Courtesy of Schimpff's Confectionary.

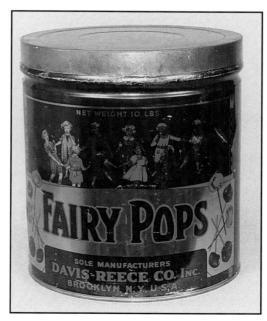

Fine Confections by Loose Wiles Co., Kansas City, marked Janssen Oster, $50.00 – 75.00. Courtesy of Joan Bunte.

Fairy Pops by Davis-Reece Co. Inc., Brooklyn, New York, 10" x 9", $150.00 – 200.00. Courtesy of Schimpff's Confectionary.

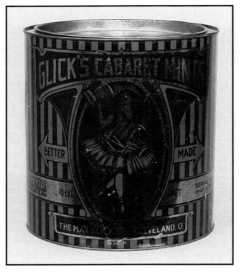

Glick's Cabaret Mints by The Max Glick Co., Cleveland, Ohio, marked Heekin Can Co., Cin. Ohio, 9¼" x 8", $150.00 – 200.00. Courtesy of Schimpff's Confectionary.

Golden Pheasant Scotch Toffee marked San Fransico, 2½" x 5¼", $25.00 – 50.00. Courtesy of Schimpff's Confectionary.

Gowdy & Carney holiday candy tin marked State Center, Iowa, 3½" x 3¾", $75.00 – 100.00. Courtesy of Schimpff's Confectionary.

Grand Union by Grand Union Tea Co., Brooklyn, New York, marked Passaic Metalware Co., 8¾" x 6" x 4", $25.00 – 50.00. Courtesy of Schimpff's Confectionary.

Gunther's Breath Perfume flat pocket, ½" x 3½" x 2¼", $25.00 – 50.00. Courtesy of Bob & Sherri Copeland.

Hard Candies by First National Stores Inc., Boston, Massachusetts, 7" x 3½" x 2¼", $25.00 – 50.00.
Courtesy of Schimpff's Confectionary.

Hardie's marked Enterprise Can Co., McKees Rocks, Pennsylvania, 10¼" x 12½", $50.00 – 75.00. Courtesy of Schimpff's Confectionary.

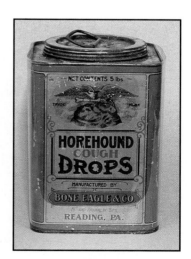

Horehound Drops by Bone, Eagle & Co., Reading, Pennsylvania, 7½" x 5" x 5", $100.00 – 150.00.
Courtesy of Schimpff's Confectionary.

Heller Holiday Mix by Heller Candy Co. Inc., Paterson, New Jersey, 8" x 5" x 5", $1.00 – 25.00.
Courtesy of Schimpff's Confectionary.

Holly Brand by Clinton-Copeland Co., Burlington, Iowa, 10½" x 7½", $25.00 – 50.00. Courtesy of Schimpff's Confectionary.

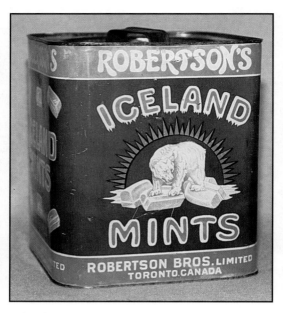

Humming Bird Brand by F.D. Seward, National Candy Co. Inc., St. Louis, 8" x 5½", $50.00 – 75.00. Courtesy of Schimpff's Confectionary.

Iceland Mints by Robertson Bros. Inc., Toronto, Canada, 7¾" x 6½" x 6½", $75.00 – 100.00. Courtesy of Richard & Ann Lehmann.

Jackie Coogan by Boston Confectionary Co., marked Canco, ¾" x 2" x 8", $25.00 – 50.00. Courtesy of Schimpff's Confectionary.

Kandies for the Kiddies lunch box marked Tindeco, 3" x 6" x 3¾", $200.00 – 250.00. Courtesy of Richard & Ann Lehmann.

Johnson's paper label by Great Eastern Candy Co. Inc., Baltimore, Maryland, 11" x 12¼", $1.00 – 25.00.

Korday by Korday Candies Inc., Brooklyn, New York, 8½" x 10½", $25.00 – 50.00. Courtesy of Schimpff's Confectionary.

Krisp Peanut Brittle by Lummis & Co., Philadelphia & Suffolk, Virginia, 8¼" x 12½", $75.00 – 100.00. Courtesy of Schimpff's Confectionary.

Liggett's Hard Candy, 4½" x 4½" x 3¼", $100.00 – 150.00. Courtesy of Tom & Mary Lou Slike.

Loft Snow Flake Mints, 3¾" x 3½", $1.00 – 25.00. Courtesy of Schimpff's Confectionary.

Log Cabin Confections by Ellis & Helfer Co., Wheeling, West Virginia, marked A.C. Co. 45A, 6½" x 6", $50.00 – 75.00. Courtesy of Schimpff's Confectionary.

McCormick's Old English Toffee by McCormick Mfg. Co., Denver, Colorado, 5¼" x 6½" x 4", $75.00 – 100.00. Courtesy of Bob & Sherri Copeland.

Mellor & Rittenhouse glass front licorice and lozenges tin marked Somers Bros., Brooklyn, New York, 7" x 5" x 5", $100.00 – 150.00. Courtesy of Schimpff's Confectionary.

Mizpah Mints by The Walter F. Ware Co., Philadelphia, ½" x 3" x 1", $1.00 – 25.00. Courtesy of Schimpff's Confectionary.

Moxie by Moxie Co. of America, ½" x 2¾" x 1¾", $50.00 – 75.00. Courtesy of Schimpff's Confectionary.

Mrs. Leland's Golden Butter-Bits by Mrs. Leland's Kitchens, Chicago, Illinois, marked 1960, 3½" x 5", $1.00 – 25.00.

Mrs. Leland's Country Store Butter-Sticks by Mrs. Leland's Kitchens, Chichago, Illinois, marked 1964, 3½" x 5", $1.00 – 25.00.

Mueller-Keller's Confections marked Missouri Can Co., 14½" x 12½", $50.00 – 75.00. Courtesy of Schimpff's Confectionary.

Necco by New England Confectionary Co., Boston, Massachusetts, marked Passaic Metalware, left: 9" x 5" x 5"; right: 6" x 4"; $25.00 – 50.00 ea. Courtesy of Schimpff's Confectionary.

Nevin's by The W.C. Nevin Candy Co., Denver, Colorado, 7½" x 6", $1.00 – 25.00. Courtesy of Schimpff's Confectionary.

Orme's Malted Milk Toffies by J. Orme & Sons Ltd., Liverpool, England, 4" x 3" x 1¼", $25.00 – 50.00. Courtesy of Bob & Sherri Copeland.

Pan Work Confections by California Peanut Co.,
Oakland, California, 3¼" x 4", $75.00 – 100.00.
Courtesy of Schimpff's Confectionary.

Parkinson's Butter Scotch by Don Parkinson,
Wins., ¾" x 4" x 3", $25.00 – 50.00. Courtesy of
Grant Smith.

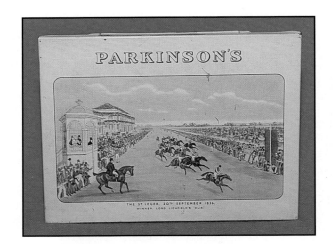

Parkinson's Butter Scotch by Parkinson & Son, made
in England, ¾" x 5¾" x 4½", $1.00 – 25.00. Courtesy of
Bob & Sherri Copeland.

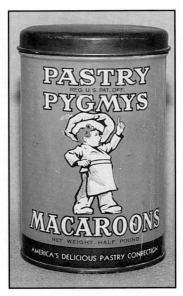

Pastry Pygmys Macaroons by
Charles F. Mattlage & Sons
Inc., New York City, 6" x 3½",
$50.00 – 75.00. Courtesy of Richard
& Ann Lehmann.

Peerless by Geo. Ziegler Co., Milwaukee, Wisconsin, marked A.C. Co. 70A, 14½" x 10", $75.00 – 100.00. Courtesy of Schimpff's Confectionary.

Peter Paul's Cream Mints by Peter Paul Candy MFG. Co. Inc., Naugatuck, Connecticut, 3" x 2½" x 1¾", $1.00 – 25.00. Courtesy of Schimpff's Confectionary.

Pilot Kisses by McAfee Candy Co., Indianapolis, Indiana, 5½" x 3½", $25.00 – 50.00. Courtesy of Schimpff's Confectionary.

Power Candy Mineralized by Granger Farms, Buskirk, New York, marked A.C. Co. 10A, 6¼" x 4" x 2¼", $25.00 – 50.00. Courtesy of Schimpff's Confectionary.

Pony Brand by Pony Brand Essence & Syrup Co. Limited, Quebec, Canada, 5¼" x 12½", $200.00 – 250.00. Courtesy of Schimpff's Confectionary.

Reed's Butter Scotch Patties by Reed Candy Co., Chicago, Illinois, $1.00 – 25.00 ea. Courtesy of Schimpff's Confectionary.

Purity Brand by Standard Candy Co., Nashville, Tennessee, 9½" x 8½", $50.00 – 75.00. Courtesy of Schimpff's Confectionary.

Repetti Caramels marked New York, 1¾" x 6" x 3¼", $1.00 – 25.00. Courtesy of Schimpff's Confectionary.

Reymers by Reymer & Brothers Inc., Pittsburgh, marked A.C. Co. 53A, 6½" x 6¾", $75.00 – 100.00. Courtesy of Schimpff's Confectionary.

Richelieu by Sprague, Warner & Co., Chicago, Illinois, 4" x 3½", $1.00 – 25.00. Courtesy of Schimpff's Confectionary.

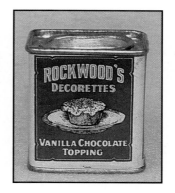

Rock Candy Drips ingredient tin by Mason Ehrman Co., Portland, Oregon, 7" x 6¾", $100.00 – 150.00. Courtesy of Wm. Morford Auctions.

Rockwood's Decorettes trial size by The Rockwood Co., Brooklyn, New York, marked A.C. Co., 2" x 1¾" x 1", $25.00 – 50.00. Courtesy of Schimpff's Confectionary.

Riverro by Bunte Bros., Chicago, marked Continental Can Co., 10" x 4½" x 4½", $1.00 – 25.00. Courtesy of Joan Bunte.

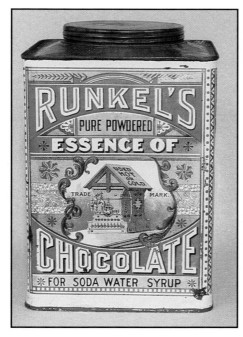

Runkel's by Runkel Bro's, New York, New York, 9½" x 6" x 6", $200.00 – 250.00.

Schabacker's Hard Candies by Buffalo-Candy Co., Buffalo, New York, marked Republic Metalware Co., Buffalo, New York, 9¼" x 5¼", $25.00 – 50.00. Courtesy of Schimpff's Confectionary.

  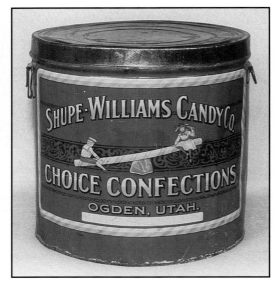

Obverse   Reverse

Sharp's Super-Kreem Toffee by Edward Sharp & Sons Ltd., England, 5" x 3¼" x 1½", $25.00 – 50.00. Courtesy of Lawson & Lin Veasey.

Shupe-Williams by Shupe Williams Candy Co., Ogden, Utah, 12" x 12½", $200.00 – 250.00. Courtesy of Schimpff's Confectionary.

Snow Drop by E.G. Whitman & Co., Philadelphia, Pennsylvania, 4¾" x 4¼", $1.00 – 25.00. Courtesy of Schimpff's Confectionary.

Sparkling Gems by Rodda Candy Co., Lancaster, Pennsylvania, 6¾" x 5¾", $25.00 – 50.00. Courtesy of Schimpff's Confectionary.

Sunshine Kisses by The Chandler & Rudd Co.,
marked A.C. Co. 52A, 7" x 9¾", $75.00 – 100.00.
Courtesy of Schimpff's Confectionary.

Up to Date by Up to Date
Candy Mfg. Co., New York,
marked Continental Can Co.,
8½" x 5" x 5", $25.00 – 50.00.
Courtesy of Schimpff's Confectionary.

White Dove Confections paper label by Zion Institutions &
Industries, Zion, Illinois, 9¼" x 12½", $1.00 – 25.00.
Courtesy of Schimpff's Confectionary.

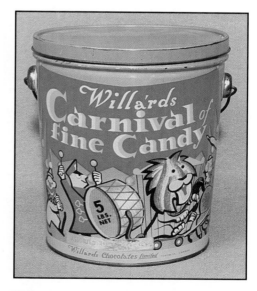

Willards by Willards Chocolates, Toronto,
Canada, 7¼" x 6½", $25.00 – 50.00. Courtesy
of Schimpff's Confectionary.

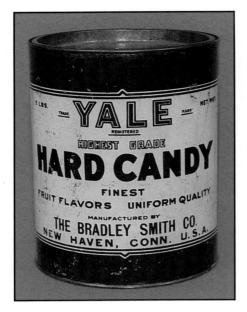

Young's marked Philadelphia, Pennsylvania, right: 3½" x 6", $25.00 – 50.00; left: 3¾" x 2¼" x 2¾", $1.00 – 25.00. Courtesy of Schimpff's Confectionary.

Yale by The Bradley Smith Co., New Haven, Connecticut, marked Bertels Metalware Co., Kingston, Pennsylvania, 7¾" x 6¼", $25.00 – 50.00. Courtesy of Schimpff's Confectionary.

Zig-Zag confection cup by The D.L. Clark Co., Pittsburgh, Pennsylvania, 1" x 1¾", $50.00 – 75.00.

Zig-Zag, Home of Washington, by D.L.C. Confections, 1" x 2½", $25.00 – 50.00. Courtesy of Bob & Sherri Copeland.

Zingo Sweets by Euclid Candy Co., marked Tindeco, 8¼" x 10¼", $150.00 – 200.00. Courtesy of Schimpff's Confectionary.

Asco Brand by American Stores Co., Philadelphia, Pennsylvania, 4½" x 3¾" x 2¼", $100.00 – 150.00. Courtesy of Hoby & Nancy Van Deusen.

Baby Stuart by Sprague, Warner & Co., Chicago, Illinois, 6" x 3½" x 2½", $150.00 – 200.00. Courtesy of Buffalo Bay Auction Co.

Barker Breakfast by J.H. Barker & Co., New York, 4½" x 2½" x 2½", $50.00 – 75.00. Courtesy of Hoby & Nancy Van Deusen.

Beacon cardboard with tin top and bottom, 8" x 4" x 3", $50.00 – 75.00. Courtesy of Buffalo Bay Auction Co.

Benefit Breakfast paper label by The Benefit Co. & Direct Importing Co. Inc., 4¼" x 3¼" x 2¼", $1.00 – 25.00. Courtesy of Hoby & Nancy Van Deusen.

Big Master by Big Master Cocoa Co., Bay City, Michigan, 8" x 4" x 3", $150.00 – 200.00. Courtesy of Buffalo Bay Auction Co.

Bischoff's by F. Bischoff Chocolate and Cocoa Works, Brooklyn, New York, 3" x 2", $50.00 – 75.00. Courtesy of Buffalo Bay Auction Co.

Blooker's paper label by Blooker's Cocoa Works, Amsterdam, Holland, 6¼" x 3½", $25.00 – 50.00. Courtesy of Hoby & Nancy Van Deusen.

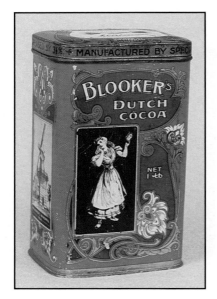

Blooker's Dutch Cocoa by L.C. Blooker, Amsterdam, Holland, 6" x 3½" x 2¾", $50.00 – 75.00. Courtesy of Hoby & Nancy Van Deusen.

Blue Mill cardboard with tin top and bottom, 8" x 4" x 3", $50.00 – 75.00. Courtesy of Buffalo Bay Auction Co.

Breakfast Cocoa by H.O. Wilber & Sons, Philadelphia, New York, marked Somers Bros., Brooklyn, New York, 5" x 2½" x 2½", $75.00 – 100.00 ea. Courtesy of Hoby & Nancy Van Deusen.

Court House by C.F. Smith Co., Detroit, Michigan, $50.00 – 75.00. Courtesy of Buffalo Bay Auction Co.

Capitol by The Andrus-Scofield Co., Columbus, Ohio, 6" x 3" x 3", $75.00 – 100.00. Courtesy of Bob & Sherri Copeland.

Brimfull by Kitchen Products Inc., Chicago, Illinois, 9¾" x 4½" x 3", $50.00 – 75.00. Courtesy of Buffalo Bay Auction Co.

De Beste Cacao by Driessen, Rotterdam, 5¼" x 3" x 2¼", $1.00 – 25.00. Courtesy of Hoby & Nancy Van Deusen.

Elkay paper label by Klein & Co., 5" x 2¾", $1.00 – 25.00. Courtesy of Tom & Mary Lou Slike.

Fry's by J.S. Fry & Sons, Bristol & London, left: 6½" x 3" x 3", $50.00 – 75.00; right: 6" x 3" x 3", $25.00 – 50.00. Courtesy of Hoby & Nancy Van Deusen.

Guittard by Guittard Chocolate Co., San Francisco, California, marked A.C. Co. 94A, 6½" x 3", $1.00 – 25.00. Courtesy of Schimpff's Confectionary.

Hooton's by Hooton Cocoa & Chocolate Co., Newark, New Jersey, marked Passaic Metalware, Passaic, New Jersey, 4¾" x 2½" x 2½", $25.00 – 50.00. Courtesy of Hoby & Nancy Van Deusen.

Index Brand by Montgomery Ward & Co., 5¾" x 3½" x 3½", $100.00 – 150.00. Courtesy of Hoby & Nancy Van Deusen.

Klein's sample 1¾" x 1½" x ¾", $150.00 – 200.00. Courtesy of Wm. Morford Auctions.

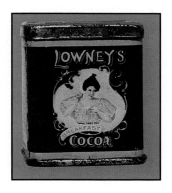

Lowney's sample, 1½" x 1¼" x ¾", $200.00 – 250.00. Courtesy of Wm. Morford Auctions.

Klein's by Klein Chocolate Co. Inc., Elizabethtown, Pennsylvania, 8¾" x 6¾", $25.00 – 50.00. Courtesy of Hoby & Nancy Van Deusen.

McCobb's by H. McCobb, New York, 5" x 2½" x 2½", $200.00 – 250.00. Courtesy of Alex & Marilyn Znaiden.

Miller's Gold Medal paper label by George Miller & Son Co., Philadelphia, 3½" x 2½", $100.00 – 150.00. Courtesy of Hoby & Nancy Van Deusen.

National by Geo. Rasmussen Co., 5" x 2½" x 2½", $200.00 – 250.00. Courtesy of Bob & Sherri Copeland.

Pette marked Wormerveer-Holland, 3½" x 2" x 2", $100.00 – 150.00. Courtesy of Wm. Morford Auctions.

Premier by Francis H. Leggett & Co., New York, New York, 9¾" x 4½" x 3", $25.00 – 50.00. Courtesy of Bob & Sherri Copeland.

Rawleigh's sample by The W.T. Rawleigh Co., Freeport, Illinois, 1¾" x 1¼" x ½", $100.00 – 150.00. Courtesy of Wm. Morford Auctions.

Rawleigh's by W.T. Rawleigh Co., Freeport, Illinois, 6" x 3¼" x 2½", $25.00 – 50.00. Courtesy of Bob & Sherri Copeland.

Rose's Ceylon by Cleveland Chocolate Co., Cleveland, Ohio, marked S.A. Ilsley, 4½" x 2½" x 2½", $100.00 – 150.00. Courtesy of Hoby & Nancy Van Deusen.

Silver Buckle by E.R. Godfrey & Sons Co., Milwaukee, Wisconsin, 6¼" x 3¼" x 3¼", $50.00 – 75.00. Courtesy of Hoby & Nancy Van Deusen.

Wan-Eta paper label by Massachusetts Chocolate Co., Boston, Massachusetts, 4" x 2½" x 1½", $100.00 – 150.00. Courtesy of Hoby & Nancy Van Deusen.

Ward's by Dr. Ward's Medical Co., Winona, Minnesota, 6" x 3" x 2", $50.00 – 75.00. Courtesy of Buffalo Bay Auction Co.

Wan-Eta paper label by Massachusetts Chocolate Co., Boston, Massachusetts, 7" x 4", $150.00 – 200.00. Courtesy of Tom & Mary Lou Slike.

Whitman's Instantaneous by Stephen F. Whitman & Son Inc., Philadelphia, 5" x 4½" x 3", $100.00 – 150.00. Courtesy of Hoby & Nancy Van Deusen.

Winner by Wabash Baking Powder Co., Wabash, Indiana, 6" x 3¼" x 3¼", $50.00 – 75.00. Courtesy of Bob & Sherri Copeland.

COCOANUT TINS

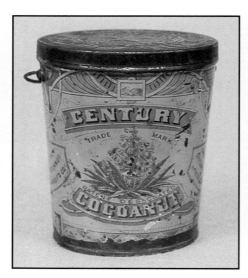

Brunswick by Warner & Merritt, Philadelphia, marked Ginna & Co., 5¼" x 2½" x 2½", $100.00 – 150.00. Courtesy of Hoby & Nancy Van Deusen.

Century by The Cocoanut Mfg. Co., New York, 3¾" x 3¼", $150.00 – 200.00. Courtesy of Hoby & Nancy Van Deusen.

Clover Farm by Clover Farm Stores, Cleveland, Ohio, 3½" x 3", $75.00 – 100.00. Courtesy of Hoby & Nancy Van Deusen.

Crystallized by Metropolitan Cocoanut Co., New York, 6½" x 3¾", $100.00 – 150.00. Courtesy of Hoby & Nancy Van Deusen.

Dunham's shaker tin, 5" x 3", $50.00 – 75.00. Courtesy of Hoby & Nancy Van Deusen.

Dunham's paper label by Durham Mfg. Co., New York & St. Louis, 5¼" x 2½", $250.00 – 300.00. Courtesy of Hoby & Nancy Van Deusen.

Dunham's by Dunham Mfg. Co., St. Louis, Missouri, 4¾" x 4¼", $75.00 – 100.00. Courtesy of Hoby & Nancy Van Deusen.

Enterprise marked Ginna & Co., 6¼" x 3¼" x 3¼", $200.00 – 250.00. Courtesy of Wm. Morford Auctions.

Fairway paper label by Twin City Wholesale Grocer Co., St. Paul, Minnesota, 4" x 2¾", $50.00 – 75.00. Courtesy of Hoby & Nancy Van Deusen.

Obverse

Golden Crown by Croft & Allen, Philadelphia, marked Ginna & Co., New York, large: 6¼" x 3¼" x 3¼"; small: 5¼" x 2½" x 2½"; $150.00 – 200.00 ea. Courtesy of Hoby & Nancy Van Deusen.
Note: Reverse side is San Blas.

Reverse

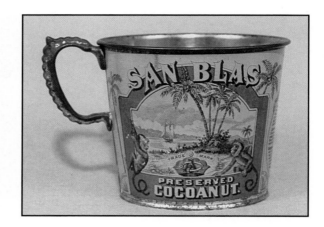

Obverse   Reverse

Golden Crown Cup by Croft & Allen, Philadelphia, Pennsylvania, 3¼" x 3¾", $200.00 – 250.00. Courtesy of Hoby & Nancy Van Deusen.

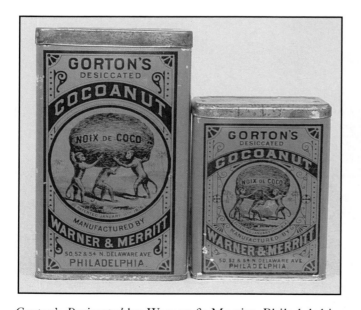

Hall Mark by Stein-Hall Mfg. Co., Chicago, Illinois, 3½" x 3", $50.00 – 75.00. Courtesy of Hoby & Nancy Van Deusen.

Gorton's Desiccated by Warner & Merritt, Philadelphia, marked Ginna & Co., New York, left: 6" x 3½" x 2½"; right: 4¼" x 3¼" x 2"; $100.00 – 150.00 ea. Courtesy of Hoby & Nancy Van Deusen.

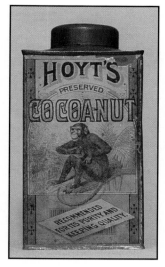

Hoyt's by Wm. Hoyt Co., marked Ginna & Co., New York, 6" x 3" x 3", $200.00 – 250.00. Courtesy of Arnold & Cindy Richardson.

I.G.A. by Independant Grocers Alliance Distributing Co., Chicago, Illinois, 3½" x 3", $50.00 – 75.00. Courtesy of Hoby & Nancy Van Deusen.

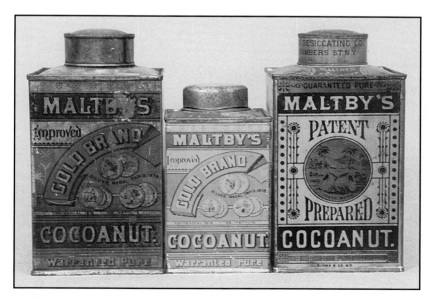

Maltby's by Maltby Desiccating Co., New York, marked Ginna & Co., New York, left & right: 6" x 3¼" x 3¼"; center: 4¾" x 2½" x 2½"; $75.00 – 100.00 ea. Courtesy of Hoby & Nancy Van Deusen.

Maltby's by Maltby Desiccating Co., New York, marked Ginna & Co., New York, 5" x 3", $25.00 – 50.00. Courtesy of Hoby & Nancy Van Deusen.

McEwan by Walter McEwan Co., Albany, New York, marked S.A. Ilsley, shows advertisement for Royal Dutch Coffee, 5¾" x 3¼" x 3¼", $400.00 – 450.00. Courtesy of Wm. Morford Auctions.

Metropolitan by Herron & Spencer, New York, 5" x 2½" x 2½", $75.00 – 100.00 ea. Courtesy of Hoby & Nancy Van Deusen.

Millars by E.B. Millar & Co., Chicago, marked Chicago Stamping Co., 6½" x 3¼" x 3¼", $200.00 – 250.00. Courtesy of Hoby & Nancy Van Deusen.

Plee-zing by George W. Simmons Corp., New York, New York, 3½" x 3", $50.00 – 75.00. Courtesy of Hoby & Nancy Van Deusen.

Schepp's marked S.A. Ilsley, 5" x 3", left: $200.00 – 250.00; right: $100.00 – 150.00. Courtesy of Hoby & Nancy Van Deusen.

Schepp's marked Somers Bros., Brooklyn, New York, 3¾" x 3½", $100.00 – 150.00.
Courtesy of Hoby & Nancy Van Deusen.

Schepp's marked S.A. Ilsley, New York, 6" x 3½" x 3½", $100.00 – 150.00. Courtesy of Hoby & Nancy Van Deusen.

Schepp's marked Kirwan & Tyler Can Co., Baltimore, Maryland, 5¾" x 3½" x 3½", $100.00 – 150.00. Courtesy of Hoby & Nancy Van Deusen.

Schepp's marked Kirwan & Tyler Can Co., Baltimore, Maryland, 4½" x 4¼", $100.00 – 150.00. Courtesy of Hoby & Nancy Van Deusen.

Schepp's marked S.A. Ilsley, 5" x 3", $250.00 – 300.00 ea. Courtesy of Hoby & Nancy Van Deusen.

Schepp's New York, marked S.A. Ilsley, 6" x 3¾" x 3¾", $100.00 – 150.00. Courtesy of Hoby & Nancy Van Deusen.

Schepp's large: 4¾" x 4½"; small: 3¾" x 3¼"; $100.00 – 150.00 ea. Courtesy of Hoby & Nancy Van Deusen.

Schepp's marked S.A. Ilsley,
5½" x 3¾" x 3¾", $100.00 –
150.00. Courtesy of Arnold & Cindy
Richardson.

Windsor paper label marked
New York, 7" x 3¾" x 2¼",
$75.00 – 100.00. Courtesy of Hoby &
Nancy Van Deusen.

Windsor paper label, 5" x 2" x 2",
$100.00 – 150.00. Courtesy of Richard & Ann
Lehmann.

3-In-One by Boyle-Midway Inc., Cranford, New Jersey, $1.00 – 25.00 ea. Courtesy of Lawson & Lin Veasey.

A-Penn by A-Penn Oil Co., Butler, Pennsylvania, 5" x 2¼" x 1¼", $25.00 – 50.00. Courtesy of Lawson & Lin Veasey.

Alemite by Stewart-Warner Corp., Chicago, Illinois, 5¼" x 2¼" x 1", $1.00 – 25.00. Courtesy of Lawson & Lin Veasey.

Allstate sold by Sears Roebuck & Co., marked Continental Can Co., 5" x 2¼" x 1", $25.00 – 50.00. Courtesy of Lawson & Lin Veasey.

Amoco by American Oil Co., 5½" x 2¼" x ¾", $25.00 – 50.00 ea. Courtesy of Lawson & Lin Veasey.

Anker by Anker Corp. of America, 5¼" x 2¼" x 1", $1.00 – 25.00. Courtesy of Lawson & Lin Veasey.

Archer by Archer Petroleum Corp., Omaha, Nebraska, 5¼" x 2¼" x 1", $25.00 – 50.00. Courtesy of Lawson & Lin Veasey.

Arrow by Arrow Petroleum Co., 4¾" x 2¼" x 1¼", $25.00 – 50.00. Courtesy of Lawson & Lin Veasey.

Bardahl by Bardahl Manufacturing Corp., Seattle, Washington, 4¾" x 2¼" x 1¼", $50.00 – 75.00. Courtesy of Lawson & Lin Veasey.

Blue Ribbon by International Metal Polish Co. Inc., Indianapolis, Indiana, 5¾" x 2¼" x 1¼", $25.00 – 50.00. Courtesy of Lawson & Lin Veasey.

Boye by The Boye Needle Co., Chicago, 4¾" x 2¼" x 1¼", $25.00 – 50.00 ea. Courtesy of Lawson & Lin Veasey.

Caltex, 6¼" x 1¾", $50.00 – 75.00. Courtesy of Lawson & Lin Veasey.

Cities Service, 6" x 2¼" x 1¼"; left: $25.00 – 50.00; right: $50.00 – 75.00. Courtesy of Lawson & Lin Veasey.

Conlube by Consumer Oil Co., New York, New York, 5½" x 2¼" x 1", $25.00 – 50.00. Courtesy of Lawson & Lin Veasey.

Cross Country by Sears, Roebuck & Co., 5¼" x 2¼" x 1", $50.00 – 75.00. Courtesy of Lawson & Lin Veasey.

E by The Carter Oil Co., 5½" x 2¼" x 1¼", $50.00 – 75.00. Courtesy of Lawson & Lin Veasey.

Emerson by The Emerson Electric Mfg. Co., St. Louis, Missouri, 3½" x 2½", $50.00 – 75.00. Courtesy of Lawson & Lin Veasey.

Esso, left: by Imperial Oil Ltd., Canada, 6¾" x 3¼" x 1¼", $25.00 – 50.00; center: by Humble Oil, Houston, Texas, 5¼" x 2¼" x 1", $1.00 – 25.00; right: by Esso Inc., U.S.A., 5" x 2¼" x 1", $1.00 – 25.00. Courtesy of Lawson & Lin Veasey.

Ever-Ready by Ever-Ready Co. Division of Plough Inc., New York & Memphis, left: 6½" x 2¼" x 3¼", $1.00 – 25.00; center: 6" x 2¼" x 1¼", $25.00 – 50.00; right: 5¼" x 2¼" x ¾", $1.00 – 25.00. Courtesy of Lawson & Lin Veasey.

Fairway by International Distributors, Memphis, Tennessee, 5¼" x 2½" x ¾", $1.00 – 25.00. Courtesy of Lawson & Lin Veasey.

Fiendoil by Cambridge & Cambridge Co., Washington, D.C., left: 3¾" x 2¼" x 1¼", $50.00 – 75.00; center: 4¾" x 2½" x 1¼", $1.00 – 25.00; right: 5" x 2½" x 1¼", $1.00 – 25.00. Courtesy of Lawson & Lin Veasey.

Firestone by The Firestone Tire & Rubber Co., Akron, Ohio, 5½" x 2½" x 1", $25.00 – 50.00. Courtesy of Lawson & Lin Veasey.

Firestone by The Firestone Tire & Rubber Co., 5¼" x 2¼" x 1", $25.00 – 50.00. Courtesy of Lawson & Lin Veasey.

Ford by Ford Motor Co., 3½" x 2¾" x 1½", $25.00 – 50.00. Courtesy of Lawson & Lin Veasey.

Gold Eagle by Gold Eagle Products Co., Chicago, Illinois, marked Canco, 5¾" x 2¼" x 1¼", $25.00 – 50.00. Courtesy of Lawson & Lin Veasey.

Gulfoil by Gulf Oil Corp., Pittsburgh, Pennsylvania, 6¼" x 2½" x 1", $1.00 – 25.00. Courtesy of Lawson & Lin Veasey.

Gulf by Gulf Oil Corp., Pittsburgh, Pennsylvania, 6½" x 2¾" x 1½", $25.00 – 50.00. Courtesy of Lawson & Lin Veasey.

Hoppe's by Frank A. Hoppe Inc., Philadelphia, Pennsylvania, 4¾" x 2¼" x 1¼", $25.00 – 50.00. Courtesy of Lawson & Lin Veasey.

Humble by Humble Oil & Refining Co., Houston, Texas, 5½" x 2¼" x 1", $50.00 – 75.00. Courtesy of Lawson & Lin Veasey.

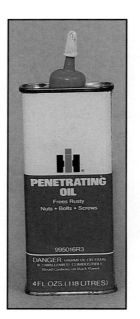

IH by International Harvester Co., Chicago, Illinois, 6" x 2" x 1", $1.00 – 25.00. Courtesy of Lawson & Lin Veasey.

Kant-Rust by Boyle Midway Inc., Jersey City, New Jersey, 5" x 2¼" x ¾", $1.00 – 25.00. Courtesy of Lawson & Lin Veasey.

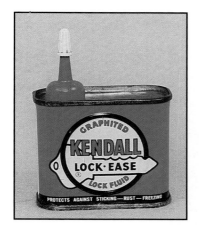

Kendall Lock-Ease by Kendall Refining Co., Bradford, Pennsylvania, marked C.C. Co., 2½" x 2¼" x 1", $1.00 – 25.00. Courtesy of Lawson & Lin Veasey.

Kendall by Kendall Refining Co., Bradford, Pennsylvania, 4" x 2¾" x 1½", $25.00 – 50.00. Courtesy of Lawson & Lin Veasey.

KF by Kaiser-Frazier, Willow Run, Michigan, 5¼" x 2¼" x 1", $75.00 – 100.00. Courtesy of Lawson & Lin Veasey.

M-F-A by M-F-A Oil Co., 4¾" x 2¼" x 1¼", $25.00 – 50.00. Courtesy of Lawson & Lin Veasey.

Many-Use by Many-Use Oil Co., New York, 4½" x 2" x 1", $25.00 – 50.00. Courtesy of Lawson & Lin Veasey.

Marathon by The Ohio Oil Co. Inc., left: 6¼" x 2¼" x 1¼", $25.00 – 50.00; center: 5½" x 2¼" x 1¼", $50.00 – 75.00; right: 5¼" x 2¼" x 1", $1.00 – 25.00. Courtesy of Lawson & Lin Veasey.

Marble's by Marble Arms & Manufacturing Co., Gladstone, Michigan, 4¾" x 2¼" x 1¼", $50.00 – 75.00. Courtesy of Lawson & Lin Veasey.

Marvel by Emerol Manufacturing Co., New York, left: 3½" x 2", $25.00 – 50.00; center: 5" x 2½" x 1¼", $50.00 – 75.00; right: 5½" x 2¼" x 1", $25.00 – 50.00. Courtesy of Lawson & Lin Veasey.

Marvel by Marvel Oil Co. Inc., Port Chester, New York, left: 6" x 2" x 1"; right: 5¼" x 2¼" x 1", $1.00 – 25.00 ea. Courtesy of Lawson & Lin Veasey.

Maytag by The Maytag Co., Newton, Iowa, 6½" x 1¾", $25.00 – 50.00. Courtesy of Lawson & Lin Veasey.

Maytag by The Maytag Co., Newton, Iowa, 4¼" x 2½", $50.00 – 75.00. Courtesy of Lawson & Lin Veasey.

Maytag by The Maytag Co., Newton, Iowa, 6½" x 3" x 1½", $25.00 – 50.00. Courtesy of Lawson & Lin Veasey.

Mobil by Socony Mobil Oil Co. Inc., 5½" x 2¼" x 1", $25.00 – 50.00. Courtesy of Lawson & Lin Veasey.

Mr. Muscles by Pyroil Co. Inc., La Crosse, Wisconsin, 5¼" x 2¼" x 1", $1.00 – 25.00. Courtesy of Lawson & Lin Veasey.

Nyoil by Wm. F. Nye Inc., New Bedford, Massachusetts, left: 5½" x 2¼" x ¾"; right: 5" x 2¼" x 1¼"; $1.00 – 25.00 ea. Courtesy of Lawson & Lin Veasey.

Mr. Shhhh by Pyroil Co. Inc., La Crosse, Wisconsin, 5¼" x 2" x ¾", $1.00 – 25.00. Courtesy of Lawson & Lin Veasey.

New Home by New Home Sewing Machine Co., Rockford, Illinois, 5¼" x 2¼" x 1", $25.00 – 50.00. Courtesy of Lawson & Lin Veasey.

O.K.'s, 5¼" x 2¼" x 1", $50.00 – 75.00. Courtesy of Lawson & Lin Veasey.

Oily Bird by Ronson Corp., Wood-Ridge, New Jersey, 6" x 2" x 1", $25.00 – 50.00. Courtesy of Lawson & Lin Veasey.

Outers by Outers Laboratories Inc., Onalaska, Wisconsin, left: 5" x 2½" x 1"; right: 5¼" x 2¼" x ¾"; $1.00 – 25.00 ea. Courtesy of Lawson & Lin Veasey.

Pecard by Pecard Chemical
Co., Green Bay, Wisconsin, 3" x
2¼" x ¾", $1.00 – 25.00. Courtesy
of Lawson & Lin Veasey.

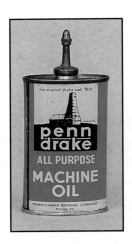

Penn Drake by Pennsylvania
Refining Co., Butler, Penn-
sylvania, 5" x 2¼" x 1¼",
$75.00 – 100.00. Courtesy of
Lawson & Lin Veasey.

Pfaff sewing machine oil,
5¼" x 2¼" x ¾", $1.00 –
25.00. Courtesy of Lawson &
Lin Veasey.

Purol by The Pure Oil Co., left: 5¼" x
2½" x 1¼", $25.00 – 50.00; right: 3½" x
2¼" x 1¼", $50.00 – 75.00. Courtesy of Lawson
& Lin Veasey

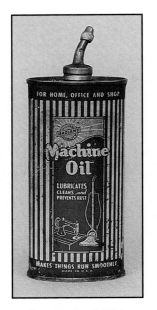

Radiant by Boyl-Midway
Inc., Jersey City, New
Jersey, 5¾" x 2¼" x 1¼",
$25.00 – 50.00. Courtesy of
Lawson & Lin Veasey.

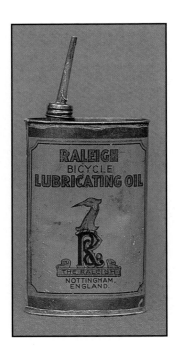

Raleigh from Nottingham,
England, 7" x 3" x 1¼",
$75.00 – 100.00. Courtesy of
Lawson & Lin Veasey.

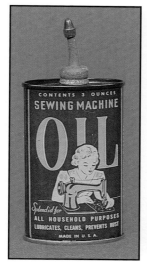

Shell by Shell Oil Co., left to right: 1 – 6" x 2¼" x 1¼", $50.00 – 75.00; 2 & 3 – 5¼" x 2¼" x 1", $25.00 – 50.00; 4 – Soap Box Derby, 6" x 2¼" x 1", $75.00 – 100.00; 5 – 5½" x 2¼" x 1", $1.00 – 25.00. Courtesy of Lawson & Lin Veasey.

Sewing Machine, 5" x 2¼" x 1¼", $1.00 – 25.00. Courtesy of Lawson & Lin Veasey.

Shamrock by Shamrock Oil and Gas Corp., Amarillo, Texas, 6" x 2½" x 1", $25.00 – 50.00. Courtesy of Lawson & Lin Veasey.

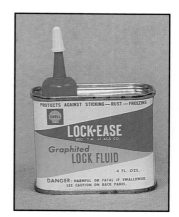

Shell Lock-Ease by Shell Oil Co., New York, 4" x 2¾" x 1½", $1.00 – 25.00. Courtesy of Lawson & Lin Veasey.

Sinclair by Sinclair Refining Co. Inc., New York, left: paper label, 6" x 2¼" x 1¼", $50.00 – 75.00; center: 6" x 2¼" x 1¼", $25.00 – 50.00; right: 5" x 2¼" x 1", $25.00 – 50.00. Courtesy of Lawson & Lin Veasey.

Singer by The Singer Manufacturing Co., left: 5¼" x 2½" x 1"; right: 3¼" x 2¼" x 1"; $1.00 – 25.00 ea. Courtesy of Lawson & Lin Veasey.

Skelly by Skelly Oil Co., 5¼" x 2¼" x 1", $50.00 – 75.00. Courtesy of Lawson & Lin Veasey.

Snow Bird, 6" x 2¼" x 1¼", $50.00 – 75.00. Courtesy of Lawson & Lin Veasey.

Standard by Standard Oil Co., left: 5¾" x 2¼" x 1¼", $25.00 – 50.00; right: 6½" x 2½" x 1", $1.00 – 25.00. Courtesy of Lawson & Lin Veasey.

Sunoco by Sun Oil Co., Philadelphia, Pennsylvania, 5¼" x 2¼" x 1", left: $25.00 – 50.00; center: $1.00 – 25.00; right: $1.00 – 25.00. Courtesy of Lawson & Lin Veasey.

Suntac by Sun Oil Co., Philadelphia & Toronto, 8" x 3", $100.00 – 150.00. Courtesy of Lawson & Lin Veasey.

Tavern by Socony-Vacuum Oil Co. Inc., marked A.C. Co. 68A, 6¼" x 2¼" x 1¼", $75.00 – 100.00. Courtesy of Lawson & Lin Veasey.

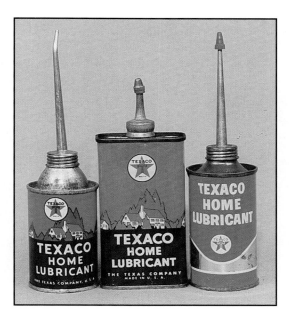

Texaco by The Texas Co., left: 6½" x 1¾", $25.00 – 50.00; center: 5½" x 2¼" x 1", $25.00 – 50.00; right: by Texaco Inc., 6½" x 1¾", $1.00 – 25.00. Courtesy of Lawson & Lin Veasey.

Texaco by The Texas Co., Arthur, Texas, 5" x 2¾" x 1¼", $100.00 – 150.00. Courtesy of Lawson & Lin Veasey.

Unico by Unico Products Co., 5½" x 2½" x 1", $1.00 – 25.00. Courtesy of Lawson & Lin Veasey.

Vickers by The Vickers Refining Co. Inc., Wichita, Kansas, 4¼" x 2¼" x 1", $50.00 – 75.00. Courtesy of Lawson & Lin Veasey.

Watkins by The J.R. Watkins Co., 4¼" x 2¾" x 1½", $25.00 – 50.00. Courtesy of Lawson & Lin Veasey.

Wanda by Cato Oil & Greese Co., Oklahoma City, Oklahoma, 5¾" x 2¼" x 1¼", $25.00 – 50.00. Courtesy of Lawson & Lin Veasey.

Wanda by Cato Oil and Greese Co., Oklahoma City, Oklahoma, 5½" x 2¼" x 1", $1.00 – 25.00. Courtesy of Lawson & Lin Veasey.

Whiz Stazon by R.M. Hillingshead Corp., Camden, New Jersey & Toronto, Canada, 4¼" x 2¾" x 1¼", $25.00 – 50.00. Courtesy of Lawson & Lin Veasey.

Whiz by R.M. Hollingshead Corp., 5½" x 2¼" x 1", $25.00 – 50.00. Courtesy of Lawson & Lin Veasey.

MARSHMALLOW TINS

Angelus by Cracker Jack Co., marked Canco, 3½" x 5½", $50.00 – 75.00. Courtesy of Arnold & Cindy Richardson.

Angelus by Cracker Jack Co., marked Heekin Co., 6" x 10", $50.00 – 75.00. Courtesy of Arnold & Cindy Richardson.

Apollo by F.H. Roberts Co., Boston, marked The New Can Co., Boston, Massachusetts, 2½" x 4¼", $75.00 – 100.00. Courtesy of Schimpff's Confectionary.

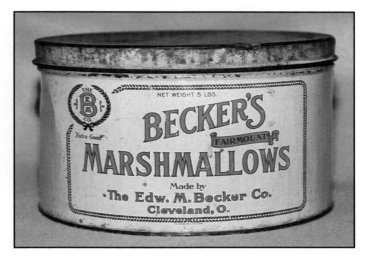

Becker's by The Edw. M. Becker Co., Cleveland, Ohio, 6" x 10", $50.00 – 75.00.

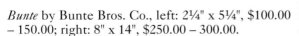

Bunte by Bunte Bros. Co., left: 2¼" x 5¼", $100.00 – 150.00; right: 8" x 14", $250.00 – 300.00.

Campfire by The Campfire Co., 3½" x 3½", $25.00 – 50.00. Courtesy of Arnold & Cindy Richardson.

Campfire by The Campfire Co., 6" x 10", $25.00 – 50.00. Courtesy of Arnold & Cindy Richardson.

Circus Club by Harry Horne Co. Ltd., Toronto, Canada, 7" x 4¼", $200.00 – 250.00. Courtesy of Richard & Ann Lehmann.

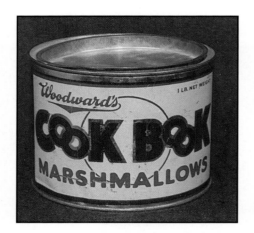

Cook Book by John G. Woodward & Co., Council Bluffs, Iowa, 4" x 5¼", $25.00 – 50.00. Courtesy of Schimpff's Confectionary.

De Luxe by De Luxe Mallow Co., Chicago-Pittsburgh, 8¼" x 12½", $150.00 – 200.00.

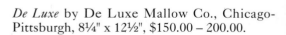
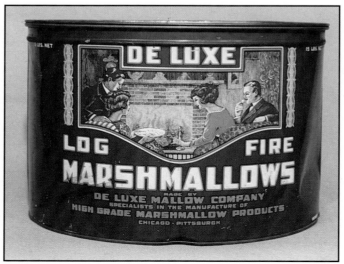

Dilling's by Dilling & Co., Indianapolis, Indiana, top: 6" x 10"; bottom: 8" x 12½"; $50.00 – 75.00 ea. Courtesy of Schimpff's Confectionary.

Fairy Queen by Loose-Wiles Co., Kansas City, 6" x 10", $25.00 – 50.00.

Heides paper label by Henry Heide, New York, 2½" x 4¼", $1.00 – 25.00. Courtesy of Schimpff's Confectionary.

Hickok's by The C.F. Hickok Co., Sidney, Ohio, 8¼" x 12½", $50.00 – 75.00. Courtesy of Mitch Morganstern.

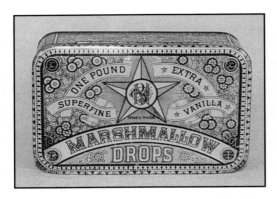

Marshmallow Drops marked Ginna & Co.,
New York, 2½" x 6" x 3¾", $75.00 – 100.00.
Courtesy of Bob & Sherri Copeland.

Monarch paper label by Reid, Murdoch & Co., Chicago, Illinois,
$75.00 – 100.00. Courtesy of Buffalo Bay
Auction Co.

Moonlight Mellos by The Patterson Candy Co., Toronto,
Canada, marked MacDonald Mfg. Co., 5" x 10½",
$75.00 – 100.00. Courtesy of Schimpff's Confectionary.

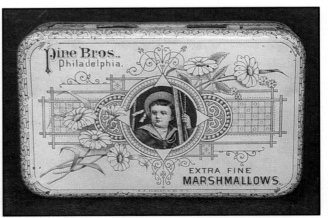

Pine Bros. marked Philadelphia, $75.00 – 100.00. Courtesy of
Schimpff's Confectionary.

Obverse

Reverse

Princess by Greylock Candy Co., Cambridge, Massachusetts, marked Heekin Can Co., 6" x 10", $50.00 – 75.00. Courtesy of Schimpff's Confectionary.

Royal by The Rochester Candy Works, Rochester, New York, marked A.C. Co. 12A, 6" x 10¼", $50.00 – 75.00. Courtesy of Schimpff' Confectionary.

Sterling by The Redel Candy Corp., Milwaukee, Wisconsin, 6" x 10", $50.00 – 75.00. Courtesy of Arnold & Cindy Richardson.

Whittle's by Whittles Inc., marked Heekin Co., 6" x 10", $50.00 – 75.00. Courtesy of Arnold & Cindy Richardson.

Unicy by Brandle & Smith Ludens Inc., $50.00 – 75.00. Courtesy of Arnold & Cindy Richardson.

NEEDLE TINS

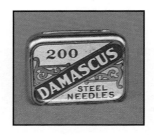

Crowley's, ½" x 1½" x 1¼", $25.00 – 50.00. Courtesy of Bob & Sherri Copeland.

Damascus, ½" x 1½" x 1¼", $25.00 – 50.00. Courtesy of Bob & Sherri Copeland.

Cali made in Germany, ¼" x 1¾" x 1¼", $25.00 – 50.00.

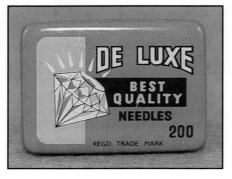

De Luxe Extra Loud made in India, ¼" x 1¾" x 1¼", $25.00 – 50.00.

De Luxe by Needle Industries (India) Ltd., ½" x 1¾" x 1¼", $25.00 – 50.00.

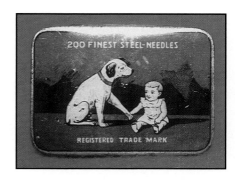

Dog & Baby made in Germany, ¼" x 1¾" x 1¼", $25.00 – 50.00. Courtesy of Tom & Lynne Sankiewicz.

Dog & Baby made in Germany, ½" x 1½" x 1¼", $25.00 – 50.00.

Dog & Radio, ½" x 1¾" x 1¼", $50.00 – 75.00. Courtesy of Richard & Ann Lehmann.

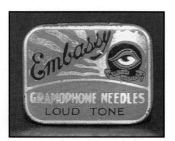

Edison Bell, ½" x 1½" x 1¼", $25.00 – 50.00.

Elite, ½" x 1¾" x 1¼", $50.00 – 75.00. Courtesy of Richard & Ann Lehmann.

Embassy by The British Needle Co. Ltd., Redditch, England, ½" x 1½" x 1¼", $25.00 – 50.00.

Favorite-Record, ½" x 1½" x 1¼", $75.00 – 100.00.

Feinste marked Schweizerfabrikat Laut, ½" x 1½" x 1¼", $25.00 – 50.00. Courtesy of Richard & Ann Lehmann.

Fortissmo marked Swiss Made, ¼" x 1¾" x 1½", $25.00 – 50.00.

Herold-Electro Tonmeister, ½" x 1¾" x 1¼", $25.00 – 50.00. Courtesy of Richard & Ann Lehmann.

Herold-Nadeln made in Germany, ¼" x 1½" x 1½", $50.00 – 75.00. Courtesy of Bob & Sherri Copeland.

His Masters Voice by Victor Talking Machines Co., Camden, New Jersey, ¾" x 2¼" x 1¾", $50.00 – 75.00. Note: A smaller size exists with less value.

His Masters Voice (soft tone) by The Gramophone Co. Ltd., ½" x 1½" x 1¼", $25.00 – 50.00.

His Masters Voice (half tone) by The Gramophone Co. Ltd., ½" x 1½" x 1¼", $25.00 – 50.00.

His Masters Voice, ½" x 2½" x 1½", $50.00 – 75.00 ea. Courtesy of Dave Garland.

Leading Always British tin, ½" x 1½" x 1¼", $25.00 – 50.00.

Leola made in Germany, ½" x 1¾" x 1¼", $50.00 – 75.00.

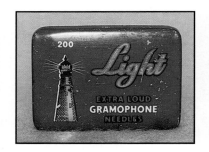

Light, ¼" x 1¾" x 1¼", $25.00 – 50.00.

Marschall made in Germany, ½" x 2¼" x 1¼", $25.00 – 50.00.

Marschall made in Germany, ½" x 1½" x 1¼", $25.00 – 50.00.

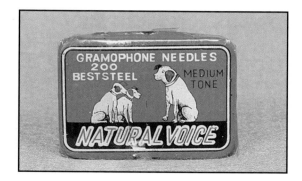

Natural Voice, ¼" x 1¾" x 1¼", $25.00 – 50.00.

Parrot made in Hong Kong, ¼" x 2" x 1¼", $1.00 – 25.00. Courtesy of Tom & Lynne Sankiewicz.

Pegasus made in Germany, ¼" x 1¾" x 1¼", $25.00 – 50.00.

Prym 555 made in Germany, ½" x 1¾" x 1¼", $50.00 – 75.00.

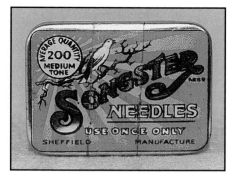

Songster by J. Stead & Co. Ltd., Sheffield, England, ¼" x 1¾" x 1¼", $25.00 – 50.00.

Songster by J. Stead & Co. Ltd., Sheffield, ¼" x 1¾" x 1¼", $25.00 – 50.00.
Note: Various colors exist.

Taj Mahal, ¼" x 1¾" x 1¼", $25.00 – 50.00.

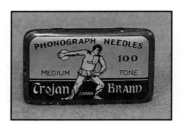

Trojan Brand made in Japan, ¼" x 1¾" x 1", $50.00 – 75.00. Courtesy of Bob & Sherri Copeland.

Verona, ¼" x 1½" x 1½", $25.00 – 50.00.

Victrola by Victor Talking Machine Co., Camden, New Jersey, $1.00 – 25.00. Courtesy of Dave Garland.

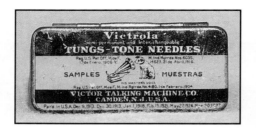

Victrola by Victor Talking Machine Co., Camden, New Jersey, ¼" x 2" x 1", $25.00 – 50.00. Courtesy of Tom & Lynne Sankiewicz.

Winett Gold, ½" x 1¾" x 1¼", $1.00 – 25.00.

PEANUT BUTTER TINS

Acorn by Bayle Food Products, St. Louis, Missouri, 3½" x 4", $100.00 – 150.00. Courtesy of Tom & Mary Lou Slike

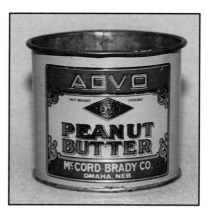

Advo by McCord Brady Co., Omaha, Nebraska, 3½" x 3½", $100.00 – 150.00. Courtesy of Richard & Ann Lehmann.
Note: A handle is attached to reverse side.

Beaver Brand by Beaver Maple Products, Whitby, Ontario, 3" x 4", $600.00 – 700.00.
Courtesy of Grant Smith.

Bishop's by Bishop & Co., Los Angeles & San Diego, California, $50.00 – 75.00.

Browne's Pedigreed by Pedigreed Products Corp., Elmira, New York, 4" x 3¼", $200.00 – 250.00.

Dixie High Grade by The Kelly Co., Cleveland, Ohio, 3½" x 4", $100.00 – 150.00. Courtesy of Tom & Mary Lou Slike.

Frontenac by Gannon Grocery Co., Marquette, Michigan, marked A.C. Co. 54A, 3½" x 3", $25.00 – 50.00. Courtesy of Bob & Sherri Copeland.

Gold Arrow by The Newton Tea & Spice Co., Cincinnati, Ohio, 3½" x 4", $150.00 – 200.00. Courtesy of Tom & Mary Lou Slike.

Happy Home by Schwabacher Bros., Seattle, 3¾" x 3¼", $400.00 – 450.00. Courtesy of Wm. Morford Auctions.

Krisp by Lummis & Co., Philadelphia, Pennsylvania, 4" x 3½", $75.00 – 100.00. Courtesy of Buffalo Bay Auction Co.

Light House by National Grocer Co., Detroit, Michigan, 3½" x 3¾", $250.00 – 300.00. Courtesy of Grant Smith.

Luncheon by Rose Field Packing Co., Alameda, California, 2¼" x 2¾", $300.00 – 350.00. Courtesy of Wm. Morford Auctions.

Obverse　　　　　　　　　Reverse

MacLaren's by MacLaren Wright Ltd., Toronto & Montreal, 3½" x 3¾", $350.00 – 400.00. Courtesy of Roy and Lynne Moseman.

Majestic by Imperial
Spice Co., Hamilton,
Ontario, Canada, 3½" x
4", $250.00 – 300.00.

Marwin by Marwin Products Co., Marion,
Ohio, 3¾" x 3¾", $50.00 – 75.00. Courtesy of
Tom & Mary Lou Slike.

Meadow Sweet by Meadow Sweet
Cheese Mfg. Co. Ltd., Montreal,
Canada, 3½" x 3¾", $100.00 – 150.00.
Courtesy of Roy & Lynne Moseman.

Monadnock by The Holbrook Grocery
Co., Keene, New Hampshire, marked
A.C. Co. of Mass., Ohio, 3½" x 3¾",
$250.00 – 300.00. Courtesy of Roy & Lynne
Moseman.

Norva by Old Dominion Peanut Corp., Norfolk, Virginia, 3½" x 3¾", $100.00 – 150.00.
Courtesy of Tom & Mary Lou Slike.

Old Tyme by Canadian Maple Products Ltd.,
Toronto, marked MacDonald Mfg. Co., 3½" x
3½", $100.00 – 150.00. Courtesy of Roy & Lynne Moseman.

Pallas by Ridenour Baker Grocery Co., Kansas City, Missouri, marked Missouri Can Co., 4¼" x 3¾", $100.00 – 150.00. Courtesy of Tom & Mary Lou Slike.

Oz by Swift & Co., Chicago, Illinois, 6" x 6¼", $25.00 – 50.00.

Palmetto by P. Duff & Sons Inc., Pittsburgh, Pennsylvania, marked Southern Can Co., Barton, Missouri, 3½" x 3½", $75.00 – 100.00. Courtesy of Roy & Lynne Moseman.

Palmetto by P. Duff & Sons Inc., Pittsburgh, Pennsylvania, 3½" x 3¼", $75.00 – 100.00. Courtesy of Tom & Mary Lou Slike.

Planters, two pound Canadian tin, 4¾" x 4¼", $400.00 – 450.00. Courtesy of Wm. Morford Auctions.

Red Seal Brand by The Newton Tea & Spice Co., Cincinnati, Ohio, 3" x 3", $50.00 – 75.00. Courtesy of Tom & Mary Lou Slike.

Royal Club by Lang & Co., Portland, Oregon, marked A.C. Co. 54A, 3½" x 3¾", $200.00 – 250.00. Courtesy of Roy & Lynne Moseman.

School Boy by The Rogers Co., Seattle, Washington, 2½" x 4", $200.00 – 250.00. Courtesy of Wm. Morford Auctions.

School Days by United Fig & Date Co., Chicago & New York, 3½" x 4", $300.00 – 350.00. Courtesy of Grant Smith.

St. Laurent's by St. Laurent Bros. Inc., Bay City, Michigan, 3½" x 3¾", $75.00 – 100.00. Courtesy of Tom & Mary Lou Slike.

White Clover by The Amos-James Grocer Co., St. Louis, Missouri, 3¾" x 3½", $600.00 – 700.00. Courtesy of Buffalo Bay Auction Co.

Wilson's Certified by Wilson & Co., Chicago, Illinois, 3½" x 3", $150.00 – 200.00. Courtesy of Wm. Morford Auctions.

POWDER TINS

Allen's Royal face powder by Allen Perfumer, New York & Plainfield, New Jersey, 1½" x 3" x 3", $75.00 – 100.00. Courtesy of Grant Smith.

Almond Meal by Frederick Loeser Co., Brooklyn, 4¾" x 2", $75.00 – 100.00. Courtesy of Grant Smith.

American Ideal by California Perfume Co., New York, 4¾" x 2½" x 1¼", $600.00 – 700.00. Courtesy of Grant Smith.

Amrico Violet by American Drug Mfg. Co. Inc., St. Louis, Missouri, 5½" x 3" x 1", $100.00 – 150.00. Courtesy of Buffalo Bay Auction Co.

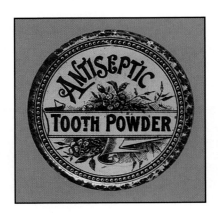

Antiseptic tooth powder, ¾" x 2½", $100.00 – 150.00. Courtesy of Wm. Morford Auctions.

Ashley's Lavender marked Ashley, New York, 3¾" x 3½" x 1¼", $25.00 – 50.00. Courtesy of Buffalo Bay Auction Co.

176

Babeskin by Babeskin Soap Co., New York, marked American Can Co. 11A., 4¾" x 1¾", no price available. Courtesy of Grant Smith.

Bambin by Bambin Laboratories, Bruxelles, 5" x 2½" x 1¼", $75.00 – 100.00.

Bathtreat, manufacturer unknown, 5½" x 2¾" x 1¾", no price available. Courtesy of Grant Smith.

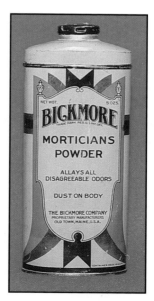

Bokara marked Vosburg, Chicago, 4½" x 2½" x 1½", no price available. Courtesy of Grant Smith.

Bickmore by The Bickmore Co., Old Town, Maine, 6¼" x 2½" x 1½", $25.00 – 50.00. Courtesy of Bob & Sherri Copeland.

Bismoline by Bismoline Mfg. Co., Lancaster, Pennsylvania, 4¾" x 2½" x 1¼", $150.00 – 200.00. Courtesy of Grant Smith.

Carbolic tooth powder, 1" x 2¼", $450.00 – 500.00. Courtesy of Wm. Morford Auctions.

Brewer's Antiseptic marked A.C. Co. 70A, 5½" x 2", $100.00 – 150.00. Courtesy of Grant Smith.

Budda by The Bonheur Co., Syracuse, New York, 5½" x 2", $75.00 – 100.00. Courtesy of Buffalo Bay Auction Co.

Butterfly by A.P. Babcock's, New York, 6" x 2" x 1½", $50.00 – 75.00. Courtesy of Bill & June Mason.

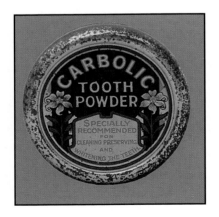

Carbolic tooth powder , 1" x 2¼", $100.00 – 150.00. Courtesy of Wm. Morford Auctions.

Corson's Violet embossed tin by Soverein Perfumers, Toronto, 4½" x 2¼" x 1¾", $50.00 – 75.00. Courtesy of Bill & June Mason.

Cream of Milk by Gustave E. Spiltoir, Long Island, New York, 5½" x 2½" x 1¼", $150.00 – 200.00. Courtesy of Mike & Sharon Hunt.

Creta Creme by Creta Creme Co., New York, 4¾" x 2½" x 1¼", $25.00 – 50.00. Courtesy of Bob & Sherri Copeland.

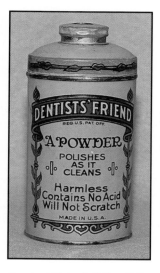

Dentists' Friend, 4½" x 2¼" x 1¾", $25.00 – 50.00. Courtesy of Bob & Sherri Copeland.

Devotia by Mansco Perfumer, New York, 6" x 2¼" x 1¼", $100.00 – 150.00. Courtesy of Bill & June Mason.

Dr. Hand's by The Hand Medicine Co., Philadelphia, Pennsylvania, 4" x 1¾", $200.00 – 250.00. Courtesy of Grant Smith.

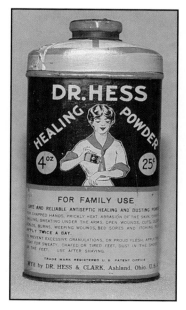

Dr. Hess healing powder by Dr. Hess & Clark, Ashland, Ohio, 5½" x 2¾", $25.00 – 50.00.

Dr. Stanley's Le Pourdre de Talc by Frasier Thornton & Cie, Cookshire, Quebec, Canada, $400.00 – 450.00. Courtesy of Buffalo Bay Auction Co.

Duchess Violet embossed tin by Eugene Lambert, Paris, France, 4¾" x 2¼" x 1¾", $25.00 – 50.00. Courtesy of Bill & June Mason.

Empress sample by Empress Powder Co., New York, New York, 2½" x 2¼" x ¾", $400.00 – 450.00. Courtesy of Wm. Morford Auctions.

Finest Talcum, man-
ufacturer unknown,
4" x 1¾", $100.00 –
150.00. Courtesy of
Grant Smith.

Florida Rose by
Bo-Kay Perfume
Co., New York,
New York & Jack-
sonville, Florida,
marked Tindeco,
6½" x 2¼" x 1¼",
$50.00 – 75.00.
Courtesy of Bob & Sherri
Copeland.

Freeman's cardboard with tin top and bottom
by The Freeman Perfume Co., Cincinnati,
Ohio, 3¾" x 4¼", $100.00 – 150.00.

French's Sweet Chimes
by French Cave &
Co. Manufacturing
Chemists, Philadel-
phia, 4" x 1¾", $100.00
– 150.00. Courtesy of Grant
Smith.

Gardenia Sweet Pea
marked Lander,
New York, 7¾" x
1¾" x 1¾", $25.00
– 50.00. Courtesy of
Bob & Sherri Copeland.

Garwood's by Schandein
& Lind, Philadelphia,
marked American Stop-
per Co., Brooklyn, New
York, 4" x 1¾", $150.00 –
200.00. Courtesy of Grant
Smith.

Gold Cross foot powder,
4½" x 2½" x 1¼",
$150.00 – 200.00. Courtesy
of Wm. Morford Auctions.

Harmony Rose by Harmony Perfumers, Toronto, Canada, 4¾" x 2½" x 1½", $75.00 – 100.00. Courtesy of Buffalo Bay Auction Co.

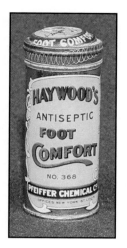

Haywood's foot powder by Pfeiffer Chemical Co., 4" x 1¾", $50.00 – 75.00. Courtesy of Grant Smith.

Hinds sample by A.S. Hinds, Portland, Maine, 2¼" x 1½" x ¾", $100.00 – 150.00.

Household borated talcum by Minnesota Pharmaceutical Mfg. Co., St. Paul, Minnesota, marked A.C. Co. 70A, 4" x 1¾", $100.00 – 150.00. Courtesy of Grant Smith.

Imperial by Imperial Talc Co., New York, 4¾" x 2½" x 1¼", $25.00 – 50.00.

Jergens Rose De Lorme by The Andrew Jergens Co., $100.00 – 150.00. Courtesy of Buffalo Bay Auction Co.

Note: A cardboard variation exists.

Jergens Crushed Lilac by The Andrew Jergens Co., 3½" x 4¼" x 1¾", $50.00 – 75.00.

Jergens Crushed Lilac by Andrew Jergens Co., 5½" x 3" x 1½", $50.00 – 75.00.

Jess paper label with glass bottom and tin top by Wm. H. Brown & Bro. Co., Baltimore, Maryland, 5" x 2½", $75.00 – 100.00. Courtesy of Grant Smith.

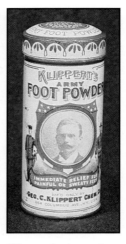

Klippert's Army foot powder by Geo. C. Klippert Chemical Co., New York, 4" x 1¾", $200.00 – 250.00. Courtesy of Grant Smith.

Lavender Talc marked Langlois, Boston, 5½" x 3" x 1", $1.00 – 25.00. Courtesy of Bill & June Mason.

Lorna Gay, 6" x 2" x 1¾", $1.00 – 25.00. Courtesy of Bob & Sherri Copeland.

Mansco baby talc by Mansco Perfumer, New York, 6" x 2¼" x 2¼", $250.00 – 300.00. Courtesy of Wm. Morford Auctions.

Marcelle by Marcelle Cosmetics Inc., Chicago, Illinois, 6" x 3" x 1½", $1.00 – 25.00. Courtesy of Mike & Sharon Hunt.

Maroc by Maroc Co., Oak Park, Illinois, 5" x 2", $25.00 – 50.00. Courtesy of Mike & Sharon Hunt.

Melba, 5" x 2½" x 2½", $400.00 – 450.00. Courtesy of Wm. Morford Auctions.

Moon Kiss diamond shaped by Page Perfumer, New York, 6" x 2½" x 1¾", $50.00 – 75.00. Courtesy of Bill & June Mason.

Neo-Dex by M.A. Wright Co., Brooklyn, New York, 5¼" x 1¾", $25.00 – 50.00. Courtesy of Mike & Sharon Hunt.

No-O-Dor by No-O-Dor Co. Inc., Johnstown, Pennsylvania, 5¾" x 2" x 2", $75.00 – 100.00. Courtesy of Mike & Sharon Hunt.

Nyal's Eas'em foot powder by New York & London Drug Co., 4½" x 2½" x 1½", $25.00 – 50.00. Courtesy of Bob & Sherri Copeland.

Page Corylopsis by Page Perfumer, New York, 5¼" x 3" x 1½", $100.00 – 150.00.

Paxtine by The Comfort Powder Co., Boston, Massachusetts, 3¼" x 1¾" x 1¾", $75.00 – 100.00. Courtesy of Grant Smith.

Prosser's Queen Corylopsis paper label by Elmer O. Prosser, Bethlehem, Pennsylvania, 4¾" x 2½" x 1½", no price available. Courtesy of Grant Smith.

Rhine Violets (No. 4711) by Mulhers & Kropff, New York, 4½" x 2½" x 1¼", $25.00 – 50.00. Courtesy of Bob & Sherri Copeland.

Rose by California Perfume Co., New York, 4½" x 2½" x 1¼", $250.00 – 300.00. Courtesy of Wm. Morford Auctions.

Royal by The Merrill Co., Toronto, Canada, 5" x 2½" x 1¼", $700.00 – 800.00. Courtesy of Bob & Sherri Copeland.

Royal Cherry Buds by Paul Rieger & Co., marked American Stopper Co., 4" x 1½", $75.00 – 100.00. Courtesy of Bob & Sherri Copeland.

Satin Skin by Albert F. Wood, Detroit, Michigan, 5" x 5¼", $250.00 – 300.00. Courtesy of Wm. Morford Auctions.

Select Lilac by Adolph Spiehler, Rochester, New York, 4¾" x 2½" x 1½", $50.00 – 75.00. Courtesy of Buffalo Bay Auction Co.

Shake-In-Your-Sox by Bellward Manufacturing Co., New York, 4¼" x 2½" x 1½", $100.00 – 150.00. Courtesy of Alex & Marilyn Znaiden.

Spencer by Spencer Perfume Co., New York and South Bend, 6" x 2¼" x 1¼", $300.00 – 350.00. Courtesy of Mike & Sharon Hunt.

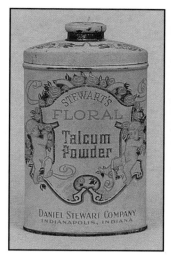

Stewart's Floral by Daniel Stewart Co., Indianapolis, Indiana, 5½" x 3" x 1½", $200.00 – 250.00. Courtesy of Mike & Sharon Hunt.

Suprema Violet by Stearns Perfumer, Detroit, Michigan, 4¾" x 2½" x 1½", $75.00 – 100.00. Courtesy of Buffalo Bay Auction Co.

Talcum and Toilet, manufacturer unknown, 4" x 1¾", $50.00 – 75.00. Courtesy of Grant Smith.

Taylor's Infants-Delight marked American Can Co., $100.00 – 150.00. Courtesy of Buffalo Bay Auction Co.

Toketa face powder marked Holman, Chicago, 1½" x 3" x 3", $50.00 – 75.00. Courtesy of Grant Smith.

Val Dona, 4½" x 2½" x 1½", $500.00 – 600.00. Courtesy of Wm. Morford Auctions.

Terriff's by Terriff & Co., Portland, Michigan, 5¾" x 2¼", $200.00 – 250.00. Courtesy of Grant Smith.

Vanta by Vanta Laboratories, Newton, Massachusetts, 5½" x 2¼", $75.00 – 100.00. Courtesy of Mike & Sharon Hunt.

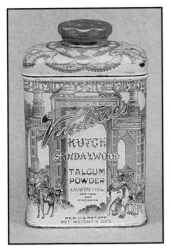

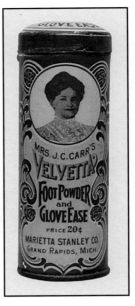

Vantine's Kutch Sandalwood by A.A. Vantine & Co., New York & Yokohama, 4½" x 2½" x 1½", $300.00 – 350.00. Courtesy of Grant Smith.

Vantine's Sana-Dermal by A.A. Vantines & Co., New York, marked Manhattan Can Co., New York, 4¾" x 2½" x 1¼", $400.00 – 450.00. Courtesy of Grant Smith.

Velvetta by Marietta Stanley Co., Grand Rapids, Michigan, 3½" x 1¼", $200.00 – 250.00. Courtesy of Wm. Morford Auctions.

Violet of the Nile marked Palmolive, 6" x 2" x 1¼", $25.00 – 50.00. Courtesy of Bob & Sherri Copeland.

Vogue Royale by Vogue Perfumery Co., New York, 4¾" x 2½" x 1¼", $350.00 – 400.00. Courtesy of Grant Smith.

White Lily by Pure Soap & Toilet Co., Tiffin, Ohio, marked American Stopper Co., 4" x 1¾", $75.00 – 100.00. Courtesy of Bob & Sherri Copeland.

Wing's Salicylated Talcum by Frederick F. Ingram & Co., Detroit, Michigan, 4" x 1¾", $100.00 – 150.00. Courtesy of Grant Smith.

Wisteria by Ho-Ro-Co Mfg. Co., St. Louis, Missouri, 8½" x 2", $150.00 – 200.00. Courtesy of Wm. Morford Auctions.

Artie's by Artie's Food Products Co., Indianapolis, Indiana, 11½" x 7½", $25.00 – 50.00. Courtesy of Mike & Sharon Hunt.

Ballreich's by Ballreich's Bros. Inc., Tiffin, Ohio, 11½" x 7½", $25.00 – 50.00. Courtesy of Mike & Sharon Hunt.

Charles by Musser's Potato Chips Inc., Mountville, Pennsylvania, 9¾" x 8½", $1.00 – 25.00.

Chesty by Chesty Foods Inc., Terre Haute, Indiana, 11½" x 7½", $75.00 – 100.00. Courtesy of Mike & Sharon Hunt. Note: A reproduction exists that measures 9¾" x 8¼".

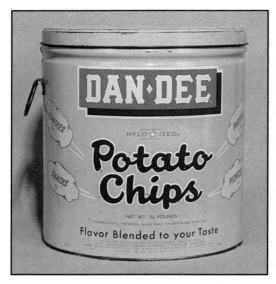

Dan-Dee by Dan-Dee Pretzel & Potato Chip Co., Cleveland, Ohio, 11" x 10", $1.00 – 25.00.

Donaldson's packed for Donaldson Baking Co. & Sterling Baking Co., 9¼" x 8½", $1.00 – 25.00.

Flaherty's by Flaherty's Potato Chip Co., Akron, Ohio, 15" x 12½", $25.00 – 50.00.

Gordon's by Gordon Foods Inc., 11½" x 7½", $50.00 – 75.00. Courtesy of Mike & Sharon Hunt.

Hiland by Hiland Potato Chip Co., 11½" x 7½", $1.00 – 25.00.

Jake's by Drennon Food Product's, Atlanta, Georgia, 11½" x 7½", $50.00 – 75.00. Courtesy of Mike & Sharon Hunt.

Jane Parker by The Great Atlantic & Pacific Tea Co. Inc., New York, New York, 9½" x 8¼", $1.00 – 25.00.

Lay's by H.W. Lay & Co. Inc., 11½" x 7½", $1.00 – 25.00.

New Era by Nicolay Dancey Inc., Detroit, Michigan, 11¼" x 7½", $1.00 – 25.00.

Num Num by Num Num Foods Inc., Cleveland, Ohio, 11½" x 7½", $75.00 – 100.00. Courtesy of Mike & Sharon Hunt.

Red Dot by Red Dot Foods Inc., Madison, Wisconsin, 11½" x 7½", $25.00 – 50.00. Courtesy of Mike & Sharon Hunt.

Salem by K.T. Salem Inc., Cleveland & Akron, Ohio, 8" x 7½", $1.00 – 25.00.

Salem's by K.T. Salem Inc., Akron, Ohio, 15½" x 12½", $25.00 – 50.00.

Scott's by Potato Products Corp., East Grand Forks, Minnesota, 11½" x 7½", $50.00 – 75.00. Courtesy of Mike & Sharon Hunt.

Top-er's by Top-er's Food Products Inc., Toledo, Ohio, 11½" x 7½", $100.00 – 150.00. Courtesy of Mike & Sharon Hunt.

Up-to-Date by Up-To-Date Food Products Co., Norwood, Ohio, 11½" x 7½", $25.00 – 50.00. Courtesy of Mike & Sharon Hunt.

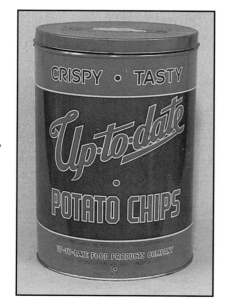

Anker shaving stick marked Dobbelman, Nijmegan, Holland, 3½" x 1½", $25.00 – 50.00. Courtesy of Dave Garland.

Antiseptic Ready Shaver safety razor marked Sicherheits, 2½" x 1½", $200.00 – 250.00. Courtesy of Don Perkins.

Bello sharpening paste by Bello Corp., Gardner, Massachusetts, ¼" x 1", $1.00 – 25.00. Courtesy of Don Perkins.

Best safety razor made in Germany, 1¾" x 2¼" x 1¼", $300.00 – 350.00. Courtesy of Don Perkins.

Blue Beard razor hone by Droescher, marked American Stopper Co., ½" x 5½" x 2¼", $75.00 – 100.00.

Bryso safety razor made in Germany, 1" x 2½" x 2", $250.00 – 300.00. Courtesy of Don Perkins.

CP shaving sticks by California Perfume Co., New York, 3½" x 1½", $25.00 – 50.00 ea. Courtesy of Dave Garland.

Cappi shave stick marked Cheramy, Paris, 3¼" x 1½", $25.00 – 50.00. Courtesy of Dave Garland.

Challenge safety razor by Challenge Cutlery Corp., marked Somers Bros., Brooklyn, New York, ½" x 2" x 1½", $400.00 – 450.00. Courtesy of Don Perkins.

Continental German safety razor by Carl Schmidt, 1½" x 3½" x 2", $150.00 – 200.00. Courtesy of Don Perkins.

Corso (American Model) safety razor made in Germany, 2½" x 1½", $1,000.00 – 1,250.00. Courtesy of Dave Garland.

Dee-Esse shave stick by Druggist Specialities Ltd., Hendon, London, 3½" x 1½", $25.00 – 50.00. Courtesy of Dave Garland.

Dr. Blair's shave stick by Blair Laboratories, Lynchburg, Virginia, 3¼" x 1½", $25.00 – 50.00. Courtesy of Dave Garland.

Electric safety razor by Friedmann & Lauterjung, ¾" x 6½" x 1¼", $300.00 – 350.00. Courtesy of Wm. Morford Auctions.

Everybody's razor tin by Everybody's Safety Razor Co., New York, $200.00 – 250.00. Courtesy of Bob & Sherri Copeland.

Erasmic shave stick, 3½" x 1¼", $25.00 – 50.00. Courtesy of Dave Garland.

Fairy safety razor, 2½" x 1½", $1,250.00 – 1,500.00. Courtesy of Wm. Morford Auctions.

Gillette blade tin by Gillette Safety Razor Co., Boston, Massachusetts, ½" x 2¼" x 1¼", $400.00 – 450.00. Courtesy of Wm. Morford Auctions.

Fripp's shave stick by Christr, Thomas & Bros. Ltd., Bristol, 3½" x 1½", $50.00 – 75.00. Courtesy of Dave Garland.

Gibbs save sticks by P. Thibaud & Co., Paris; left; 3½" x 1½", $1.00 – 25.00; right; 2" x 1¼", $25.00 – 50.00. Courtesy of Dave Garland.

Graham's shave stick by Graham Bros. & Co., Chicago, marked A.C. Co. 70A, 3¼" x 1½", $25.00 – 50.00. Courtesy of Dave Garland.

Henckels razor blade case by J.A. Henckels, ¼" x 2¼" x 1¼", $100.00 – 150.00. Courtesy of Don Perkins.

Home safety razor by Eastman & Krauss Razor Co., New York, 1¼" x 2¾" x 1½", $500.00 – 600.00. Courtesy of Don Perkins.

Imperial shave stick by Talcum Puff Co., New York, 3¼" x 1¼", $75.00 – 100.00. Courtesy of Dave Garland.

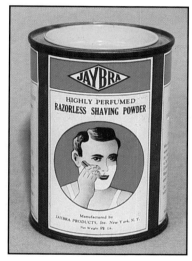

Jaybra shaving powder by Jaybra Products Inc., New York, 4¼" x 3", $1.00 – 25.00. Courtesy of Dave Garland.

Jeyes' shaving soap, 3¼" x 1½", $25.00 – 50.00. Courtesy of Dave Garland.

Keen Kutter razor hone by Simmons Hardware Co. Inc., ½" x 5½" x 2¼", $50.00 – 75.00. Courtesy of Don Perkins.

195

Klaverblade's shave stick marked Scheerstaaf No. 5013, Harlem, Holland, 3½" x 1½", $75.00 – 100.00. Courtesy of Don Perkins.

Langlois used razor blade retainer marked Liggett's, A.C. Co. 10A, 2½" x 2½" x 1¾", $25.00 – 50.00. Courtesy of Dave Garland.

Larkin cardboard stick by Larkin Co. Chemists, Buffalo, New York, 3¼" x 1½", $1.00 – 25.00. Courtesy of Dave Garland.

Le Petit safety razor by Roth & McEvoy Inc., Brooklyn, New York, ½" x 2" x 1½", $150.00 – 200.00. Courtesy of Don Perkins.

Magna safety razor, Pat. Jan. 14, 1902, 2" x 1¾" x 1¼", $350.00 – 400.00. Courtesy of Don Perkins.

Magic shaving powder by The Shaving Powder Co., Savannah, Georgia, $25.00 – 50.00.

Mohican razor blade case, ¼" x 2¼" x 1¼", $250.00 – 300.00.

Mulcuto razor sharpener by Mulcuto Mfg. Co., London, 2¼" x 2" x ¾", $200.00 – 250.00. Courtesy of Don Perkins.

Palmolive used razor blade retainer by Colegate-Palmolive-Peet Co., 2½" x 2½" x 1½", $25.00 – 50.00. Courtesy of Lawson & Lin Veasey.

Rapide safety razor with slide opening, 1¼" x 4½" x 2", $200.00 – 250.00. Courtesy of Don Perkins.

Rawleigh's shave stick by W.T. Raleigh Co., Freeport, Illinois, 3½" x 1½", $1.00 – 25.00. Courtesy of Dave Garland.

Remington cardboard shave stick with tin bottom, 3" x 1½", $1.00 – 25.00. Courtesy of Dave Garland.

Resinol shave stick by Resinol Chemical Co., Baltimore, Maryland, 3¼" x 1½", $25.00 – 50.00. Courtesy of Don Perkins.

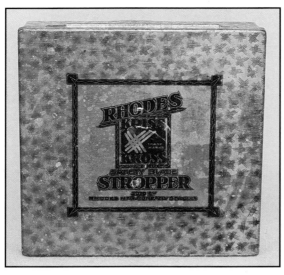

Rhodes Kriss Kross razor blade sharpener by Rhodes Mfg. Co., St. Louis, 1¾" x 4½", $50.00 – 75.00. Courtesy of Don Perkins.

Safe Tee shave stick by American Safe Tee Soap Corp., New York, 3¼" x 1½", $25.00 – 50.00. Courtesy of Dave Garland.

Solingen German razor blade case by Friedr. Herder & Son, ½" x 2¼" x 1¼", $75.00 – 100.00. Courtesy of Don Perkins.

Tarantella sharpening paste, ¼" x 1", $1.00 – 25.00. Courtesy of Don Perkins.

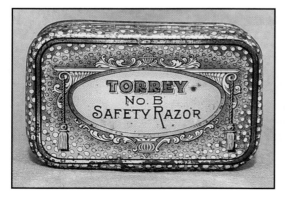

Weck's strop dressing by Edward Weck & Son Inc., New York & Brooklyn, 1¾" x 1¼", $1.00 – 25.00. Courtesy of Dave Garland.

Torrey No. B safety razor by J.R. Torrey, Worchester, Massachusetts, 1¼" x 3½" x 2¼", $300.00 – 350.00. Courtesy of Don Perkins.

Winchester safety razor marked A.C. Co. 11A, 2¾" x 1½", $700.00 – 800.00.
Courtesy of Don Perkins.

Winner safety razor, 2¼" x 1½", $1,000.00 – 1,250.00.
Courtesy of Don Perkins.

SPICE TINS

Anthracite by Goeser & Jacobs, Hazleton, Pennsylvania, 3" x 2¼" x 1¼", $150.00 – 200.00. Courtesy of Alex & Marilyn Znaiden.

Arbuckles' by Arbuckle Bros., 3½" x 2¼" x 1¼", $25.00 – 50.00. Courtesy of Mike & Sharon Hunt.

Bacon Stickney's by Bacon Stickney & Co., 11½" x 9" x 7½", $450.00 – 500.00. Courtesy of Wm. Morford Auctions.

Ben-Hur by Coffee Products of America Inc., Los Angeles & San Diego, California, 3¾" x 2¼" x 1¼", $1.00 – 25.00 ea.

Barrus marked Ginna & Co., New York, 11" x 7" x 7", $700.00 – 800.00. Courtesy of Alex & Marilyn Znaiden.

Blackbird cardboard with tin top and bottom made in Lincoln, Nebraska, $50.00 – 75.00. Courtesy of Buffalo Bay Auction Co.

Burma cardboard with tin top and bottom by Empire Spice Mills, Chicago, Illinois, 3¼" x 2¼" x 1½", $1.00 – 25.00.

Burr Mills marked S.A. Ilsley, 9½" x 8½" x 7", $150.00 – 200.00. Courtesy of Wm. Morford Auctions.

Chapin by Chapin Grocery Specialities Co., Springfield, Massachusetts, 3" x 2¼" x 1¼", $75.00 – 100.00. Courtesy of Alex & Marilyn Znaiden.

Colburn by R.T. French Co., Philadelphia, Pennsylvania, 3½" x 2¼" x 1¼", $1.00 – 25.00. Courtesy of David Morris.

Colonial by F.B. Matthews & Co. Inc., Kingston, New York, 4" x 2¼", 1¼", $75.00 – 100.00. Courtesy of Grant Smith.

Columbia by Sutherland & McMillan Co., Pittston, Pennsylvania; left: 3¾" x 2¼" x 1¼"; right; 3" x 2¼" x 1¼"; $150.00 – 200.00 ea. Courtesy of Alex & Marilyn Znaiden.

Conquest by Lewis, Hubbard & Co., Charleston, West Virginia, marked A.C. Co. 43A, 3¼" x 2¼" x 1½", $25.00 – 50.00.

Crouse's Crown by Crouse Grocery Co., Syracuse & Utica, New York, 3¾" x 2", $25.00 – 50.00. Courtesy of Grant Smith.

Crown Colony by Charter Products Co., San Francisco, California, 3¼" x 2¼" x 1¼", $1.00 – 25.00. Courtesy of David Morris.

Daisy Dell by Daisy Dell Distributors, Cincinnati, Ohio, 3" x 2¼" x 1¼", $300.00 – 350.00. Courtesy of Alex & Marilyn Znaiden.

Dye's Chili Mixture by W.A. Dye, Wichita, Kansas, 4¼" x 1½", $25.00 – 50.00.

Eagle by Bacon, Stickney & Co's Inc., Albany, New York, 3¼" x 2¼" x 1¼", $50.00 – 75.00. Courtesy of Grant Smith.

Eclipse by Western Pure Foods Ltd., Winnipeg, Canada, 3½" x 2¼" x 1¼", $50.00 – 75.00. Courtesy of Grant Smith.

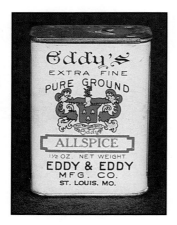

Eddy's cardboard by Eddy & Eddy Mfg. Co., St. Louis, Missouri, 3" x 2¼" x 1¼", $25.00 – 50.00. Courtesy of Grant Smith.

Elizabeth Park by S. Vogel & Sons, Hartford, Connecticut, 3¾" x 2¼" x 1¼", $100.00 – 150.00. Courtesy of Alex & Marilyn Znaiden.

Euteco cardboard with tin top and bottom by Eureka Tea Co., Chicago, Illinois, $50.00 – 75.00. Courtesy of Buffalo Bay Auction Co.

Ever-Well by Everett & Tread-well Co., Kingston, New York, 3" x 2¼" x 1¼", $100.00 – 150.00. Courtesy of Alex & Marilyn Znaiden.

Fairway by Des Moines Wholesale Grocers Co., Des Moines, Iowa, 3¼" x 2¼" x 1¼", $300.00 – 350.00. Courtesy of Alex & Marilyn Znaiden.
Note: A paper label variation exists with much less value.

Field's Quality by Henry Field Co., Shenandoah, Iowa, 3¾" x 2¼" x 1¼", $100.00 – 150.00. Courtesy of Alex & Marilyn Znaiden.

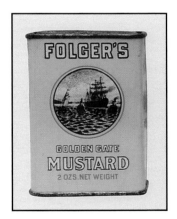

Folger's by J.A. Folger & Co., 3¼" x 2¼" x 1¼", $100.00 – 150.00. Courtesy of Wm. Morford Auctions.

Foltz Maid by The Foltz Grocery & Baking Co., Cincinnati, Ohio, 3" x 2¼" x 1¼", $200.00 – 250.00. Courtesy of Alex & Marilyn Znaiden.

Foster's cardboard with tin top and bottom by George Foster Inc., St. Paul, Minnesota, $25.00 – 50.00. Courtesy of Buffalo Bay Auction Co.

Frank's by The Frank Tea & Spice Co., Cincinnati, Ohio, 3¾" x 2", $75.00 – 100.00. Courtesy of Grant Smith.

Frank's by Frank Tea & Spice Co., Cincinnati, Ohio, 3½" x 1¼", $50.00 – 75.00. Courtesy of Richard & Ann Lehmann.

Fullarton's cardboard with tin top and bottom by F.L. Frary & Co., Minneapolis, Minnesota, 3¾" x 1¾" x 1¼", $25.00 – 50.00. Courtesy of Tom & Mary Lou Slike.

Gillett's by Sherer-Gillett Co., Chicago, Illinois, 2¼" x 1½", $25.00 – 50.00. Courtesy of Grant Smith.

Glendora by Smith & Horton Co., Warren, Pennsylvania, 3¾" x 2", $25.00 – 50.00. Courtesy of Bob & Sherri Copeland.

Gold Medal paper label by The Tracy & Avery Co., Mansfield, Ohio, 3½" x 2½" x 1¼", $1.00 – 25.00. Courtesy of Tom & Mary Lou Slike.

Gold Standard by Codville Co. Ltd., Winnipeg, 3¼" x 2½" x ¾", $25.00 – 50.00. Courtesy of Grant Smith.

Golden Dream paper label by Betterton Coffee Co. Inc., Ashland, Kentucky, 2¾" x 2¼" x 1¼", $1.00 – 25.00. Courtesy of Bob & Sherri Copeland.

Golden West by Clossett & Devers, Portland & Seattle, Washington, marked A.C. Co., 3¾" x 2¼" x 1¼", $25.00 – 50.00. Courtesy of Grant Smith.

Grisdale by Gristede Bros. Inc., New York, 4" x 2½" x 1", $50.00 – 75.00. Courtesy of Grant Smith.

Haleeka by Geo. Bubb & Sons, Williamsport, Pennsylvania, 4" x 2¼" x 1¼", $350.00 – 400.00. Courtesy of Alex & Marilyn Znaiden.

Hatchet by The Twitchell-Champlin Co., 3¾" x 2½" x 1½", $50.00 – 75.00.

Heberling's by G.C. Heberling Co., Bloomington, Illinois, 4½" x 2¼" x 2¼", $25.00 – 50.00.

Heller's paper label by Heller's Stores, San Diego, California, 3¼" x 2¼" x 1¼", $1.00 – 25.00. Courtesy of Bob & Sherri Copeland.

Here's Howe Imperial by Geo. J. Howe Co., Grove City, Pennsylvania, 3½" x 2½" x 1¼", $75.00 – 100.00. Courtesy of Grant Smith.

Hollywood by Commercial Importing Co., Seattle-Tacoma-Portland, 3½" x 2¼" x 1¼", $25.00 – 50.00. Courtesy of Grant Smith.

Hollywood cardboard by Commercial Importing Co., Seattle, Washington, 4" x 2¼" x 1¾", $25.00 – 50.00. Courtesy of Grant Smith.

Home Brand paper label by Griggs, Cooper & Co., St. Paul, Minnesota, 3¾" x 2¾" x 1¾", $25.00 – 50.00. Courtesy of Tom & Mary Lou Slike.

Hoosier Circle by National Wholesale Grocery Co., Indianapolis, Indiana, 3" x 2¼" x 1¼", $100.00 – 150.00. Courtesy of Alex & Marilyn Znaiden.

Hoyt's by Hoyt Bros. Inc., Newark, New Jersey, 3½" x 2", $25.00 – 50.00. Courtesy of Richard & Ann Lehmann.

Imperial by Gray Manufacturing Co., Spokane, Washington, 3¼" x 2¼" x 1¼", $100.00 – 150.00. Courtesy of Alex & Marilyn Znaiden.

Jack Rose by E.T. Smith Co., Worcester, Massachusetts, 3½" x 2¼" x 1½", $25.00 – 50.00. Courtesy of Alex & Marilyn Znaiden.

Juno by McClintock-Trunkey Co., Spokane, Washington, 3¼" x 2¼" x 1¼", $75.00 – 100.00. Courtesy of Richard & Ann Lehmann.

Kato cardboard by A.J. Busch Co., Mankato, Minnesota, 3¼" x 2¼" x 1½", $75.00 – 100.00. Courtesy of Grant Smith.

Keystone by Keystone Coffee Co., San Jose, California, 3¼" x 2¼" x 1¼", $25.00 – 50.00. Courtesy of Grant Smith.

Ladies' Favorite by Heller & Perrin, Pittsburgh, Pennsylvania, 4" x 2", $150.00 – 200.00. Courtesy of Alex & Marilyn Znaiden.

Le-Hi by Lehmann, Higginson Grocer Co., Wichita, Kansas, 3¼" x 2¼" x 1½", $25.00 – 50.00. Courtesy of Bob & Sherri Copeland.

Little Boy Blue paper label by Lansing Wholesale Grocer Co., Lansing, Michigan, 2½" x 2¼" x 1¼", $25.00 – 50.00. Courtesy of Bob & Sherri Copeland.

Malkin's by W.H. Malkin Co., Vancouver, Canada, 2½" x 2¼" x 1¼", $1.00 – 25.00. Courtesy of Richard & Ann Lehmann.

Maltese Cross by Meyer Brothers Drug Co., St. Louis, 3¼" x 2¼" x 1¼", $25.00 – 50.00. Courtesy of Lawson & Lin Veasey.

Manhattan by Manhattan Products Co., St. Louis, Missouri, 3¼" x 2¼" x 1¼", $150.00 – 200.00. Courtesy of Grant Smith.

Manning's by Manning Coffee Stores, marked A.C. Co. 70A, 3¼" x 2¼" x 1¼", $50.00 – 75.00. Courtesy of Grant Smith.

Marbest by C.E. Marr, Spokane, Washington, 3¼" x 2¼" x 1¼", $25.00 – 50.00. Courtesy of Grant Smith.

Massasoit by Bonnett, Schenck & Earle Co.,
New York; left: 4" x 2½"; right: 3¼" x 2";
$200.00 – 250.00 ea. Courtesy of Alex & Marilyn
Znaiden.

McCormick by McCormick &
Co. Inc., Baltimore, Maryland
& San Francisco, California,
3¾" x 2¼" x 1¼", $1.00 –
25.00. Courtesy of Mike & Sharon Hunt.

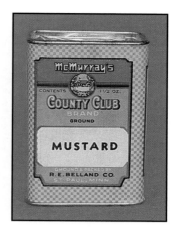

McMurray's Country Club
cardboard by R.E. Belland
Co., St. Paul, Minnesota, 3"
x 2¼" x 1¼", $1.00 – 25.00.
Courtesy of Grant Smith.

Mexene by Walker Properties Assn.,
Austin, Texas; left: 3½" x 1½", $1.00
– 25.00; right: (sample) 1¼" x 1",
$50.00 – 75.00. Courtesy of Mike & Sharon
Hunt.

Minnehaha cardboard
with tin top and bottom,
$50.00 – 75.00. Courtesy of
Buffalo Bay Auction Co.

Mixed Pickling Spices by
The Frank Tea & Spice
Co., Cincinnati, Ohio, 4" x
2", $75.00 – 100.00. Courtesy
of Grant Smith.

Mohican by Mohican Co., New York, New York, 1¾" x 2¼" x 1¼", $75.00 – 100.00. Courtesy of Grant Smith.

Mother Dawson by Kennedy Products, Gloversville, New York, 3¾" x 2½" x 1¾", $100.00 – 150.00. Courtesy of Alex & Marilyn Znaiden.

Nabob by Kelly-Douglass & Co. Ltd., Vancouver, B.C., 3¼" x 2¼" x 1¼", $25.00 – 50.00. Courtesy of Grant Smith.

Nation-Wide by Nation Wide Service Grocers, 3¼" x 2½" x 1¼", $1.00 – 25.00. Courtesy of Bob & Sherri Copeland.

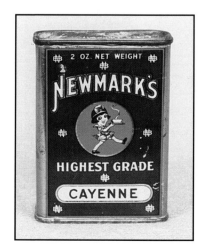

Newmark's by Newmark Bros., Los Angeles, California, 3¼" x 2½" x 1¼", $75.00 – 100.00. Courtesy of Alex & Marilyn Znaiden.

Oak Hill by E.C. Hall Co., Brockton, Massachusetts, 2¾" x 1½", $100.00 – 150.00. Courtesy of Grant Smith.

Old Mansion by C.W. Antrim & Sons, Richmond, Virginia, 4" x 2", $75.00 – 100.00.

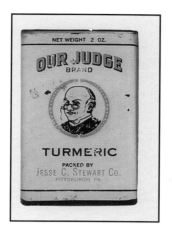

Our Judge by Jesse C. Stewart Co., Pittsburgh, Pennsylvania, $75.00 – 100.00. Courtesy of Buffalo Bay Auction Co.

Pearlicross by P.A. & S. Small Co., York, Pennsylvania, 3¾" x 2", $150.00 – 200.00. Courtesy of Alex & Marilyn Znaiden.

Pitkin's Old Home by J.M. Pitkin & Co., Newark & New York, 3¾" x 2¼" x 1¼", $50.00 – 75.00. Courtesy of Alex & Marilyn Znaiden.

Pocono by Grand Union Co., New York City, 3½" x 2¼" x 1¼", $100.00 – 150.00. Courtesy of Alex & Marilyn Znaiden.

Premium Mills by Stephen Parson's Co., Albany, New York, marked Ginna & Co., 3¼" x 2¼" x 1¼", rare, no price available. Courtesy of Wm. Morford Auctions.

Printzess by Printz &
French, Springfield,
Ohio, 3¾" x 1¼",
$75.00 – 100.00.
Courtesy of Bob & Sherri
Copeland.

Pure Quill by The Halligan
Co., Davenport, Iowa, 3½" x
2¼" x 1¼", $50.00 – 75.00.
Courtesy of Richard & Ann Lehmann.

Red Turkey by J.B. Maltby
Inc., Corning, New York,
3¾" x 2¼" x 1¼", $200.00 –
250.00. Courtesy of Alex & Marilyn
Znaiden.

Rosemary by The Cash Wholesale Grocers, Chicago, Illinois,
3" x 2¼" x 1¼", $200.00 –
250.00. Courtesy of Alex & Marilyn
Znaiden.

Royal Boy by Rasse Wholesale
Grocery Co., 3¼" x 2¼" x 1½",
$250.00 – 300.00. Courtesy of Alex
& Marilyn Znaiden.

S & F Brand by Smart & Final Co.
Wholesale Grocers, Southern California, 3¼" x 2¼" x 1¼", $100.00 –
150.00.

Selected Imported by Wixon Spice Co., Chicago, Illinois, 4" x 2", $50.00 – 75.00. Courtesy of Alex & Marilyn Znaiden.

Slade's by D & L Slade Co., Boston, Massachusetts, 2¾" x 1¾" x 1¼", $25.00 – 50.00. Courtesy of Grant Smith.

Slade's by D & L Slade Co., Boston, Massachusetts, marked A.C. Co., 4" x 1¾", $25.00 – 50.00. Courtesy of Grant Smith.

Slade's by D & L Slade Co., Boston, Massachusetts, left: 3½" x 1¾"; right: 2½" x 2¼" x 1"; $1.00 – 25.00 ea.

Smith Mole by Smith Mole & Co., Adams, Massachusetts, 3¾" x 2½" x 1½", $75.00 – 100.00. Courtesy of Alex & Marilyn Znaiden.

Stickney and Poors by Stickney and Poors Spice Co., Boston, Massachusetts, 2½" x 2¼" x 1", $25.00 – 50.00. Courtesy of Lawson & Lin Veasey.

Stickney and Poor's made in Boston, Massachusetts, $25.00 – 50.00. Courtesy of Buffalo Bay Auction Co.

Stuart's Handy by C.H. Stuart & Co., Newark, New Jersey & New York, New York; left: 4" x 2½" x 1¼"; right: 3¾" x 2¼" x 1¼"; $50.00 – 75.00 ea. Courtesy of Richard & Ann Lehmann.

Sunny Sue by J.S. Hotchkiss & Bros. Inc., Meadville, Pennsylvania, 3" x 2¼" x 1¼", $100.00 – 150.00. Courtesy of Alex & Marilyn Znaiden.

Teen Queen by The Creasey Co., Louisville, Kentucky, 2¼" x 2¼" x 1¼", $25.00 – 50.00. Courtesy of Mike & Sharon Hunt.

Three Crow by The Atlantic Spice Co., Bangor, Maine, 3¼" x 2½" x 1½", $50.00 – 75.00. Courtesy of Bob & Sherri Copeland.

Three Crow by The Atlantic Spice Co., Bangor, Maine, 3½" x 2½" x 1¼", $75.00 – 100.00. Courtesy of Buffalo Bay Auction Co.

Time O'Day by Jordan Stevens Co., Minneapolis, Minnesota, 3¼" x 2¼" x 1¼", $50.00 – 75.00. Courtesy of Grant Smith.

Travers Ship Brand paper label by Joseph Travers & Sons, London, 3" x 1", $1.00 – 25.00. Courtesy of Richard & Ann Lehmann.

Tropical cardboard by Jewett-Sherman Co., Kansas City, Missouri, 3¼" x 2¼" x 1½", $50.00 – 75.00. Courtesy of Grant Smith.

Tropical cardboard with tin top and bottom made in Milwaukee, Wisconsin, 3½" x 2¼" x 1½", $25.00 – 50.00. Courtesy of Buffalo Bay Auction Co.

Tuxedo by Tuxedo Coffee & Spice Mills Ltd., Calgary & Alberta, marked A.C. Co. 2L, 3¼" x 2½" x 1", $25.00 – 50.00. Courtesy of Grant Smith.

Tyler's by S.H. Tyler & Son, San Francisco, California, 3¼" x 2¼" x 1¼", $1.00 – 25.00. Courtesy of Grant Smith.

United paper label by United Food Sales, Milwaukee, Wisconsin, 3¼" x 2¼" x 1¼", $25.00 – 50.00. Courtesy of Grant Smith.

Valley Farm by Valley Wholesale Grocery Co., Warwick, Rhode Island & Newburgh, New York, 3¼" x 2¼" x 1¼", $75.00 – 100.00. Courtesy of Alex & Marilyn Znaiden.

Washington Club by D.J. Johnson Co. Inc., Spokane, 3¼" x 2¼" x 1¼", $25.00 – 50.00. Courtesy of Grant Smith.

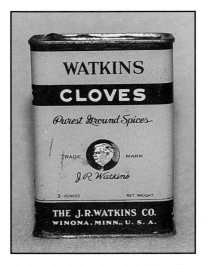

Watkins by The R.J. Watkins Co., Winona, Minnesota, 3¾" x 2½" x 1½", $1.00 – 25.00. Courtesy of David Morris.

Wellman by Wellman-Peck & Co., California, 3¾" x 2¼" x 1¼", $50.00 – 75.00. Courtesy of Richard & Ann Lehmann.

White Swan cardboard with tin top and bottom by Waples-Platter Co., Denison-Forth Worth-Dallas, Texas, 3" x 2¼" x 1½", $50.00 – 75.00. Courtesy of Mike & Sharon Hunt.

Wigwam paper label by Carpenter Cook Co., Menominee, Michigan, 3" x 2¼" x 1¼", $75.00 – 100.00. Courtesy of Grant Smith.

Wizard by Kansas Wholesale Grocer Co., Coffeyville, Kansas, marked Columbia Can Co., St. Louis, Missouri, 3¼" x 2¼" x 1¼", $100.00 – 150.00. Courtesy of Alex & Marilyn Znaiden.

Yankee Girl by Frankel's Son's, Wilkes-Barre, Pennsylvania, 3" x 1¾" x 1¼", $250.00 – 300.00. Courtesy of Alex & Marilyn Znaiden.

TEA TINS

Arbuckles' by Arbuckle Bros., Chicago, 4" x 2½" x 2½", $25.00 – 50.00. Courtesy of Bob & Sherri Copeland.

Banquet by McCormick & Co., Baltimore, Maryland, 3½" x 3" x 3", $25.00 – 50.00. Courtesy of Richard & Ann Lehmann.

Bee Brand by McCormick & Co., Baltimore, Maryland, 2" x 5" x 3¼", $25.00 – 50.00. Courtesy of Bob & Sherri Copeland.

Canova by Maury-Cole Co. Inc., Memphis-Dallas-Louisville, 3½" x 2¾" x 2¾", $25.00 – 50.00. Courtesy of Bob & Sherri Copeland.

Castle Blend by Stanley & Co., Montreal, Canada, marked Thos Davidson Mfg. Co., 7" x 6½" x 6½", $150.00 – 200.00. Courtesy of Grant Smith.

Centrella cardboard with tin top and bottom by Central Wholesale Grocers Inc., Chicago, Illinois, 3½" x 3" x 3", $50.00 – 75.00. Courtesy of Bob & Sherri Copeland.

Ceylindo by Kearley & Tonge, London, 6" x 4" x 4", $25.00 – 50.00. Courtesy of Wm. Morford Auctions.

College Girl cardboard with tin top and bottom by Jenkinson-Bode Co., Jacksonville & Beardstown, Illinois, $50.00 – 75.00. Courtesy of Buffalo Bay Auction Co.

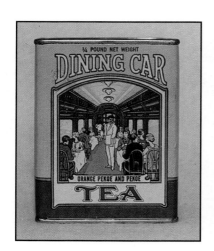

Dining Car by Norwine Coffee Co., St. Louis, Missouri, 4" x 3" x 3", $200.00 – 250.00.

Epicure by S.S. Pierce Co., Boston, Massachusetts, 5" x 3½", $25.00 – 50.00. Courtesy of Richard & Ann Lehmann.

Folger's Golden Gate by J.A. Folger & Co., San Francisco, California, 10" x 7" x 7", $300.00 – 350.00. Courtesy of Alex & Marilyn Znaiden.

Foltz Maid by Foltz Grocery & Baking Co., Cincinnati, Ohio, 4" x 2¾" x 2¾", $150.00 – 200.00 ea.

Fountain Head, ¾" x 2¼" x 2", $50.00 – 75.00. Courtesy of Grant Smith.

Gold Camel by L.H. Parke & Co., Philadelphia, ¾" x 2¼" x 2", $25.00 – 50.00. Courtesy of Bob & Sherri Copeland.

Gold Standard by The Codville Co. Limited, marked Thos Davidson Mfg. Co., Montreal, Canada, 9" x 6¾" x 4¾", $200.00 – 250.00. Courtesy of Grant Smith.

Gold Standard by The Codville Co. Limited, marked Thos Davidson Mfg. Co., Montreal, Canada, 7¾" x 7¼" x 5¼", $100.00 – 150.00. Courtesy of Grant Smith.

Golden Dome by W.S. Quinby Co., Boston & Chicago, 8" x 4", $100.00 – 150.00. Courtesy of Buffalo Bay Auction Co.

Golden Rule marked American Can Co. 70A, 9½" x 6" x 6", $25.00 – 50.00. Courtesy of Tom & Mary Lou Slike.

Hamstra's by H. Hamstra & Co., New York-Chicago, 4" x 3½" x 3½", $1.00 – 25.00. Courtesy of Richard & Ann Lehmann.

Ho-Yan by Hughes Bros. Manufacturing Co., Dallas, Texas, marked Ginna & Co., 6" x 3" x 3", $600.00 – 700.00. Courtesy of Alex & Marilyn Znaiden.

Horniman's marked London, 2¼" x 4" x 3", $25.00 – 50.00. Courtesy of Bob & Sherri Copeland.

Jack Sprat by Jack Sprat Food Inc., Marshalltown, Iowa, 5" x 2" x 2", $100.00 – 150.00. Courtesy of Buffalo Bay Auction Co.

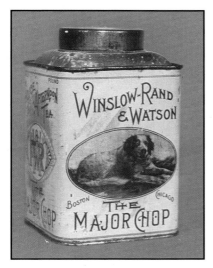

Major Chop, The by Winslow-Rand & Watson, 6" x 3½" x 3½", $200.00 – 250.00. Courtesy of Alex & Marilyn Znaiden.

Monarch (Light of Asia) by Reid, Murdoch & Co., Chicago, Illinois, 5½" x 3" x 3", $50.00 – 75.00. Courtesy of Bob & Sherri Copeland.

Monarch cardboard with tin top and bottom, by Reid, Murdock & Co., Chicago, Illinois, 3" x 3" x 3", $50.00 – 75.00. Courtesy of Richard & Ann Lehmann.

Moon Chop by The Kroger Grocery & Baking Co., Cincinnati, Ohio, 3½" x 2½" x 2", $50.00 – 75.00. Courtesy of Alex & Marilyn Znaiden.

Old Fire Side by Oakdale Mfg. Co., Providence, Rhode Island, 4¾" x 4½" x 2½", $50.00 – 75.00. Courtesy of Bob & Sherri Copeland.

Old Master by The Bour Co., 6" x 3½" x 3½", $50.00 – 75.00. Courtesy of Bob & Sherri Copeland.

Richelieu by Sprague Warner & Co., Chicago, Illinois, $1.00 – 25.00. Courtesy of Bob & Sherri Copeland.

Rosemary by Samuel Kunin & Sons Inc., Chicago, Illinois, 4½" x 2½" x 2½", $75.00 – 100.00. Courtesy of Ken & Nancy Jones.

Richelieu by Sprague Warner-Kenny Corp., Chicago, Illinois, 5¾" x 3¼" x 3¼", $1.00 – 25.00.

Royalty Chop, The, by Venslow, Runo & Watson Co., Boston, Massachusetts, 6" x 3" x 3", $25.00 – 50.00. Courtesy of Bob & Sherri Copeland.

Savoy by Steele-Wedeles Co., Chicago, 4¼" x 2½" x 2½", $75.00 – 100.00. Courtesy of Bob & Sherri Copeland.

Swain, Earle & Co's, Boston, Massachusetts, marked Ginna & Co., New York, 9" x 4¼", $200.00 – 250.00. Courtesy of Alex & Marilyn Znaiden.

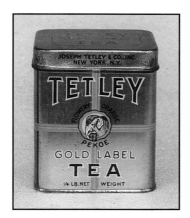

Tetley by Joseph Tetley & Co. Inc., New York, New York, 3½" x 2½" x 2¾", $1.00 – 25.00. Courtesy of Bob & Sherri Copeland.

Thurber, Whyland & Co. marked Ginna & Co., New York, 7" x 4¼", $300.00 – 350.00. Courtesy of Alex & Marilyn Znaiden.

Trapahu by Tracy, Packard & Huntoon Importers, New York, 4¾" x 3½" x 3½", $200.00 – 250.00. Courtesy of Alex & Marilyn Znaiden.

Triumph Brand, pictures Boston Tea Party, 4½" x 4½" x 2¾", $150.00 – 200.00. Courtesy of Buffalo Bay Auction Co.

Vantine's No. 19 by A.A. Vantine & Co. Inc., New York, New York, 4¾" x 2½" x 2½", $75.00 – 100.00. Courtesy of Richard & Ann Lehmann.

White Villa by White Villa Grocers Inc., Cincinnati & Dayton, Ohio, 6" x 3" x 3", $25.00 – 50.00.

AAA Brand by C.W. Hatfield Co., St. Louis, Missouri, ¾" x 2½", $1.00 – 25.00. Courtesy of Tom & Mary Lou Slike.

Addison marked Cole Stationery, Pleasantville, New Jersey, ¾" x 2½", $200.00 – 250.00. Courtesy of Tom & Mary Lou Slike.

Addo-X, manufacturer unknown, ¾" x 2", $25.00 – 50.00. Courtesy of Tom & Mary Lou Slike.

Aladdin by Aladdin Ribbon & Supply Co., Des Moines, Iowa, ¾" x 2½", $50.00 – 75.00. Courtesy of Tom & Mary Lou Slike.

Allied by Allied Carbon & Ribbon Mfg. Corp., New York, New York, ¾" x 2½", $1.00 – 25.00.

American Brand by H.M. Storms Manufacturing, New York, marked American Stopper Co., 2" x 1¾" x 1¾", $150.00 – 200.00. Courtesy of Tom & Mary Lou Slike.

Alpine by Alpine Ribbon & Carbon Co., Cleveland, Ohio, ¾" x 2½" x 2½", $50.00 – 75.00. Courtesy of Hoby & Nancy Van Deusen.

American Brand by H.M. Storms Co., New York, New York, 2" x 1¾" x 1¾", $75.00 – 100.00. Courtesy of Tom & Mary Lou Slike.

Anchor Brand by Miller & Curran Co., Chicago, Illinois, 2" x 1¾" x 1¾", $75.00 – 100.00. Courtesy of Bob & Sherri Copeland.

Armor Brand by Allen & Co., New York, New York, ¾" x 2½", $1.00 – 25.00. Courtesy of Tom & Mary Lou Slike.

Autocrat by Goldsmith Bros., New York, ¾" x 2½", $50.00 – 75.00. Courtesy of Tom & Mary Lou Slike.

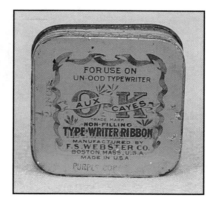

Aux Cayes OK by F.S. Webster Co., Boston, Massachusetts, ¾" x 2¼" x 2¼", $1.00 – 25.00.

Badger Brand by Chas Saltzstein & Bro., Milwaukee, Wisconsin, ¾" x 2½" x 2½", $75.00 – 100.00. Courtesy of Tom & Mary Lou Slike.

Beaver Crystal by The M.B. Cook Co., Chicago, Illinois, ¾" x 2½" x 2½", $25.00 – 50.00. Courtesy of Tom & Mary Lou Slike.

Bell by Mittag & Volger Inc., Park Ridge, New Jersey, ¾" x 2½", $1.00 – 25.00. Courtesy of Tom & Mary Lou Slike.

Benjamin Franklin by Franklin Ribbon & Carbon Co., New York, New York, ¾" x 2½", left: $25.00 – 50.00; right: $100.00 – 150.00. Courtesy of Hoby & Nancy Van Deusen.

Blue Peak by Copigraph, Limited, Great Britian, ¾" x 2½" x 2½", $25.00 – 50.00. Courtesy of Hoby & Nancy Van Deusen.

Blur Less Platinum by David L. Morrow, Pittsburgh, Pennsylvania, ¾" x 2½" x 2½", $50.00 – 75.00. Courtesy of Tom & Mary Lou Slike.

Buck-Skin by F.W. Neely Co., Chicago, Illinois, ¾" x 2½" x 2½", $50.00 – 75.00. Courtesy of Tom & Mary Lou Slike.

Bucki D & D by Buckeye Ribbon & Carbon Co., Cleveland, Ohio, ¾" x 2½", $1.00 – 25.00. Courtesy of Tom & Mary Lou Slike.

Bull-Frog by Newton-Rotherick Mfg. Co., Chicago, Illinois, ¾" x 2½" x 2½", left: $75.00 – 100.00; right: $100.00 – 150.00. Courtesy of Tom & Mary Lou Slike.

Burroughs adding machine ribbon by Burroughs Adding Machine Co., Detroit, Michigan, ¾" x 2¼" x 2¼", $25.00 – 50.00. Courtesy of Tom & Mary Lou Slike.

Cameo Brand by H.M. Storms Co., Brooklyn, New York, ¾" x 2½" x 2½", $50.00 – 75.00. Courtesy of Tom & Mary Lou Slike.

Carnation by Miller-Bryant-Pierce Co., Aurora, Illinois, ¾" x 2½" x 2½", $25.00 – 50.00. Courtesy of Tom & Mary Lou Slike.

Carter's Electric by Carter Ink Co., Boston, Massachusetts, ¾" x 2½", $1.00 – 25.00. Courtesy of Tom & Mary Lou Slike.

Carter's Inky Racer by Carter's Ink Co., 2" x 3" x 2", $300.00 – 350.00. Courtesy of Wm. Morford Auctions.

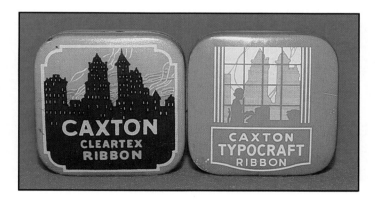

Caxton by Caxton Laboratories Inc., New York, ¾" x 2½" x 2½", left: $150.00 – 200.00; right: $75.00 – 100.00. Courtesy of Tom & Mary Lou Slike.

Challenge by Consolidated Ribbon & Carbon Co., Chicago, Illinois, left: ¾" x 2½" x 2½"; right: ¾" x 2" x 2", $25.00 – 50.00 ea. Courtesy of Tom & Mary Lou Slike.

Chesapeake by Graham Tinley & Co., ¾" x 2½" x 2½", $150.00 – 200.00. Courtesy of Hoby & Nancy Van Deusen.

Chicago Supra by Kee-Lox Mfg. Co., Chicago, Illinois, ¾" x 2½", $50.00 – 75.00. Courtesy of Tom & Mary Lou Slike.

Columbia by Columbia Ribbon Co., Cleveland, Ohio, 2" x 1¾" x 1¾", $75.00 – 100.00. Courtesy of Tom & Mary Lou Slike.

Commercial by Stenno Ribbon & Carbon Mfg. Co., ¾" x 2½", $50.00 – 75.00.

Commercial by Stenno Ribbon & Carbon Mfg. Co., Portland, Oregon, ¾" x 2½", $25.00 – 50.00. Courtesy of Tom & Mary Lou Slike.

Conquest by Quest Manufacturing Co., Chicago & New York, ¾" x 2½" x 2½", $1.00 – 25.00. Courtesy of Tom & Mary Lou Slike.

Cotton King by Pen Carbon Manifold Co., New Brunswick, New Jersey, ¾" x 2½" x 2½", $100.00 – 150.00. Courtesy of Tom & Mary Lou Slike.

Crescent by The Crescent Mfg. Co., New York, ¾" x 2½" x 2½", $100.00 – 150.00. Courtesy of Tom & Mary Lou Slike.

Crowfoot by The How Co., Old Town, Maine, 1" x 2¼" x 2¼", $25.00 – 50.00. Courtesy of Tom & Mary Lou Slike.

Curtis-Young by Curtis Young Corp., New York, New York, ¾" x 2½", $1.00 – 25.00. Courtesy of Tom & Mary Lou Slike.

Davidson by Davidson Corp., Brooklyn, New York, ¾" x 2½", $25.00 – 50.00. Courtesy of Tom & Mary Lou Slike.

De-Fi by De-Fi Manufacturing Co., New York, ¾" x 2½", $25.00 – 50.00. Courtesy of Tom & Mary Lou Slike.

De-Fi by De-Fi Manufacturing Co., New York, New York, ¾" x 2½" x 2½", $50.00 – 75.00.

Diana plastic by C. Neubauer Carbon & Ribbon Co., St. Paul & Minniapolis, Minnesota, ¾" x 2½", $1.00 – 25.00. Courtesy of Tom & Mary Lou Slike.

Ditmars by Pen Carbon-Manifold Co., New York, 2" x 1¾" x 1¾", $50.00 – 75.00. Courtesy of Tom & Mary Lou Slike.

Ditto by Ditto Inc., Chicago, Illinois, left: ¾" x 2½" x 2½"; right: ¾" x 2½"; $1.00 – 25.00 ea. Courtesy of Tom & Mary Lou Slike.

Dundee by Dundee Ribbon Co., ¾" x 2½" x 2½", $75.00 – 100.00. Courtesy of Tom & Mary Lou Slike.

Duplimat by Adressograph-Multigraph Corp., Cleveland, Ohio, ¾" x 2½", $1.00 – 25.00. Courtesy of Tom & Mary Lou Slike.

Durhess Excellence marked Remington, ¾" x 2½", $50.00 – 75.00. Courtesy of Tom & Mary Lou Slike.

Duro-Flex, ¾" x 2½", $1.00 – 25.00. Courtesy of Tom & Mary Lou Slike.

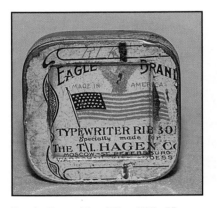

Eagle Brand by The T.I. Hagen Co., ½" x 2¼" x 2¼", $100.00 – 150.00. Courtesy of Tom & Mary Lou Slike.

Efco by Elliott-Fisher Co., Harrisburg, Pennsylvania, ¾" x 2¼" x 2¼", $1.00 – 25.00. Courtesy of Tom & Mary Lou Slike.

Elite by National Office Supply Co., Waukegan, Illinois, ¾" x 2½" x 2½", $75.00 – 100.00. Courtesy of Tom & Mary Lou Slike.

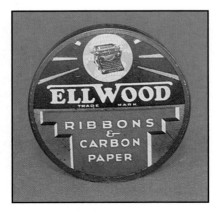

Elk Brand by Miller-Bryant-Pierce Co., Aurora, Illinois, left: ¾" x 2¼", $50.00 – 75.00; right: ¾" x 2½" x 2½", $75.00 – 100.00. Courtesy of Tom & Mary Lou Slike.

Ellwood by Underwood-Elliott-Fisher Co., ¾" x 2¼", $25.00 – 50.00. Courtesy of Tom & Mary Lou Slike.

Emerald Brand by L.C. Smith & Corona Typewriters Inc., ¾" x 2½" x 2½", $25.00 – 50.00. Courtesy of Tom & Mary Lou Slike.

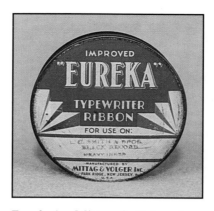

Eureka by Mittag & Volger Inc., Park Ridge, New Jersey, ¾" x 2½", $25.00 – 50.00. Courtesy of Tom & Mary Lou Slike.

Eureka by Mittag Division Burroughs Corp., Park Ridge, New Jersey, ¾" x 2½", $25.00 – 50.00. Courtesy of Tom & Mary Lou Slike.

Excello Brand by Kitko Specialty Co., Rochester, New York, ¾" x 2½" x 2½", $1.00 – 25.00. Courtesy of Bob & Sherri Copeland.

Fine Service by Stenno Ribbon & Carbon Mfg. Co., Portland, Oregon, left: ¾" x 2½", $25.00 – 50.00; right: ¾" x 2½" x 2½", $1.00 – 25.00. Courtesy of Tom & Mary Lou Slike.

Flax's by The Flax Co., Dayton, Ohio, ¾" x 2½" x 2½", $1.00 – 25.00. Courtesy of Tom & Mary Lou Slike.

Flexo by Waters & Waters Mfg. Co., Burlington, New Jersey, ¾" x 2½", $25.00 – 50.00. Courtesy of Tom & Mary Lou Slike.

Fox by Fox Typewriter Co., Grand Rapids, Michigan, ¾" x 2½" x 2½", $100.00 – 150.00. Courtesy of Tom & Mary Lou Slike.

Glider by Lerman Bros. Inc., Long Island, New York, ¾" x 2½", $100.00 – 150.00. Courtesy of Tom & Mary Lou Slike.

Globe Brand by Crown Ribbon & Carbon Mfg. Co., Rochester, New York, ¾" x 2¼" x 2¼", $75.00 – 100.00. Courtesy of Tom & Mary Lou Slike.

Gold Medal by Stenno Ribbon & Carbon Mfg. Co., Portland, Oregon, ¾" x 2½", $25.00 – 50.00. Courtesy of Tom & Mary Lou Slike.

Golden Gate by Perry & Guy, San Francisco, California, ¾" x 2½", $150.00 – 200.00. Courtesy of Hoby & Nancy Van Deusen.

Golden Poppy by H. & M.C. Co., San Francisco, California, ¾" x 2½", $75.00 – 100.00.

Gra-Dear by Graver Dearborn Corp., Chicago, Illinois, ¾" x 2½", $75.00 – 100.00. Courtesy of Tom & Mary Lou Slike.

Grand Prize by Pacific Carbon & Ribbon Mfg. Co. Inc., San Fransicisco, California, ¾" x 2½" x 2½", $50.00 – 75.00. Courtesy of Tom & Mary Lou Slike.

Great Lakes by Great Lakes Carbon Co., Cleveland, Ohio, ¾" x 2½", $50.00 – 75.00. Courtesy of Hoby & Nancy Van Deusen.

Guild by Columbia Ribbon & Carbon Mfg. Co., Glen Cove, New York, ¾" x 2½", $25.00 – 50.00. Courtesy of Tom & Mary Lou Slike.

Hallmark by Cameron Manufacturing Co., Dallas, Texas, left: ¾" x 2½" x 2½"; right: ¾" x 2½"; $1.00 – 25.00 ea. Courtesy of Tom & Mary Lou Slike.

Hammond Superior, ¾" x 2¼" x 2¼", $75.00 – 100.00. Courtesy of Tom & Mary Lou Slike.

Harlee by Harlee Ribbon & Carbon Co., New York, New York, ¾" x 2½", $25.00 – 50.00. Courtesy of Tom & Mary Lou Slike.

Higbee by The Higbee Co., Cleveland, Ohio, ¾" x 2½" x 2½", $1.00 – 25.00. Courtesy of Tom & Mary Lou Slike.

Hub by F.S. Webster Co., Boston, Massachusetts, ¾" x 2½" x 2½", $1.00 – 25.00. Courtesy of Tom & Mary Lou Slike.

Imperial by Tom Lawrence Office Supplies, Michigan, ¾" x 2½", $1.00 – 25.00. Courtesy of Tom & Mary Lou Slike.

Imperial Easy Copy by Peerless Imperial Co. Inc., Newark, New Jersey, ¾" x 2½", $25.00 – 50.00. Courtesy of Tom & Mary Lou Slike.

International Telephone by International Telephone & Telegraph Corp., ¾" x 2½" x 2½", $100.00 – 150.00. Courtesy of Tom & Mary Lou Slike.

Invincible by American Writing Machine Co., New York, 1¾" x 2" x 1¾", $25.00 – 50.00. Courtesy of Tom & Mary Lou Slike.

Invincible by American Writing Machine Co., New York, New York, ¾" x 2½", $25.00 – 50.00.

Just-Rite by Allen & Co., New York, New York, ¾" x 2½" x 2½", $25.00 – 50.00. Courtesy of Tom & Mary Lou Slike.

Kabella Bell Brand by Bell Brand Products, ¾" x 2½", $50.00 – 75.00. Courtesy of Tom & Mary Lou Slike.

Klean Type by Willson Stationery Co. Ltd., Canada, ¾" x 2½", $1.00 – 25.00.

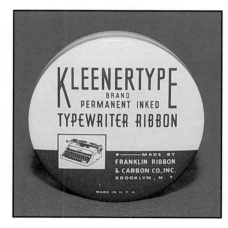

Kleenertype by Franklin Ribbon & Carbon Co. Inc., Brooklyn, New York, ¾" x 2½", $25.00 – 50.00.

Kodye by The Randall Co., Cincinnati, Ohio, ¾" x 2½", $1.00 – 25.00. Courtesy of Tom & Mary Lou Slike.

Kreko by Kress Stores, left: ¾" x 2½", $1.00 – 25.00; center: ¾" x 2½", $25.00 – 50.00; right: ¾" x 2½" x 2½", $1.00 – 25.00. Courtesy of Tom & Mary Lou Slike.

L.C. Smith (horses) by L.C. Smith & Bros., 1¾" x 2" x 1¾", $75.00 – 100.00. Courtesy of Tom & Mary Lou Slike.

Longhorn by American Carbon Paper Mfg. Co., Ennis, Texas, ¾" x 2½", $25.00 – 50.00.

M & M by Mittag & Volger Inc., Park Ridge, New Jersey, ¾" x 2½", $1.00 – 25.00 ea. Courtesy of Tom & Mary Lou Slike.

M.B.P. Brand by Miller-Bryant-Pierce Co., Aurora, Illinois, ¾" x 2½", $25.00 – 50.00. Courtesy of Tom & Mary Lou Slike.

Madame Butterfly by Miller-Bryant-Pierce, Aurora, Illinois, ¾" x 2½", $1.00 – 25.00.

Manhattan by Manhattan Stationery Co. Inc., New York, ¾" x 2½", $150.00 – 200.00. Courtesy of Tom & Mary Lou Slike.

Maple Leaf by Underwood Limit-ed, Canada, 1" x 2½", $25.00 – 50.00.

Maple Leaf by United Typewriter Co. Ltd., Canada, ¾" x 2¼" x 2¼", $25.00 – 50.00.

Marvello, manufacturer unknown, ¾" x 2½", $1.00 – 25.00. Courtesy of Tom & Mary Lou Slike.

McCrory's Vanderbilt, ¾" x 2½" x 2½", $1.00 – 25.00. Courtesy of Tom & Mary Lou Slike.

McGregor made in Washington, D.C., ¾" x 2½", left: $50.00 – 75.00; right: $1.00 – 25.00. Courtesy of Tom & Mary Lou Slike.

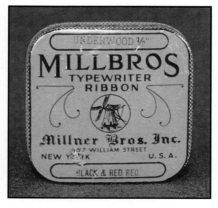

Medallion by Miller-Bryant-Pierce, Aurora, Illinois, 1" x 2½", $25.00 – 50.00.

Millbros by Millner Bros. Inc., New York, New York, ¾" x 2½" x 2½", $25.00 – 50.00. Courtesy of Tom & Mary Lou Slike.

Milo by Milo Ribbon & Carbon Corp., Penn Yan, New York, ¾" x 2½" x 2½", $25.00 – 50.00. Courtesy of Tom & Mary Lou Slike.

Miracle Nylon by Mittag & Volger Inc., Park Ridge, New Jersey, ¾" x 2½", $25.00 – 50.00. Courtesy of Tom & Mary Lou Slike.

Monogram by Underwood, Elliott, Fisher Co., Burlington, New Jersey, ¾" x 2½", $25.00 – 50.00. Courtesy of Tom & Mary Lou Slike.

Mountain Brand marked Idaho Typewriter Exchange, ¾" x 2½", $75.00 – 100.00. Courtesy of Tom & Mary Lou Slike.

Natural Bridge by Caldwell-Sites Co., Roanoke, Virginia, ¾" x 2½" x 2½", $100.00 – 150.00. Courtesy of Tom & Mary Lou Slike.

No Name Checkerboard stock tin, ¾" x 2½", $25.00 – 50.00. Courtesy of Tom & Mary Lou Slike.

No Name Compass stock tin marked Kautz Stationery Co., Indianapolis, Indiana, ¾" x 2½", $50.00 – 75.00. Courtesy of Tom & Mary Lou Slike.

No Name Gold Rose plastic stock tin marked Robert F. Wolf Co., Freemont, Ohio, 1" x 2¾", $1.00 – 25.00. Courtesy of Tom & Mary Lou Slike.

No Name Keyboard stock tin (left is cardboard), ¾" x 2½", $1.00 – 25.00 ea. Courtesy of Tom & Mary Lou Slike.

No Name Lady Spinning (oval), ¾" x 2½", $75.00 – 100.00. Courtesy of Tom & Mary Lou Slike.

No Name Office stock tin marked Utica Office Supply Co. Inc., ¾" x 2½", $25.00 – 50.00.

No Name Ship stock tin, ¾" x 2½", $50.00 – 75.00. Courtesy of Hoby & Nancy Van Deusen.

No Name Southern Belle stock tin, ¾" x 2½", $50.00 – 75.00. Courtesy of Tom & Mary Lou Slike.

No Name Tulips marked Kee-Lox Manufacturing Co., Rochester, New York, ¾" x 2½", $1.00 – 25.00. Courtesy of Tom & Mary Lou Slike.

Official by Snelling & Son, Brooklyn, New York, ¾" x 2½" x 2½", $1.00 – 25.00. Courtesy of Tom & Mary Lou Slike.

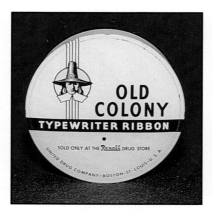

Ohashi's by H. Ohashi & Co., New York, New York, ¾" x 2½" x 2½", $25.00 – 50.00. Courtesy of Tom & Mary Lou Slike.

Old Colony by United Drug Co., Boston & St. Louis, ¾" x 2½", $25.00 – 50.00. Courtesy of Tom & Mary Lou Slike.

Old Dutch by Waters & Waters Mfg. Co., Burlington, New Jersey, ¾" x 2½", $75.00 – 100.00. Courtesy of Tom & Mary Lou Slike.

Old Dutch Line by Waters & Waters Mfg. Co., Burlington, New Jersey, ¾" x 2½" x 2½", $75.00 – 100.00. Courtesy of Tom & Mary Lou Slike.

Old English by Waters Mfg. Co., ¾" x 2½", $50.00 – 75.00.

Old Town by Old Town Ribbon & Carbon Co. Inc., Brooklyn, New York, ¾" x 2½", $50.00 – 75.00. Courtesy of Tom & Mary Lou Slike.

Old Town Dawn by Old Town Ribbon & Carbon Co. Inc., Brooklyn, New York, ¾" x 2½" x 2½", $100.00 – 150.00. Courtesy of Hoby & Nancy Van Deusen.

Panama Ink Control by Manifold Supplies Co., Brooklyn, New York, ¾" x 2½" x 2½", $25.00 – 50.00. Courtesy of Tom & Mary Lou Slike.

Park Avenue by Royal Typewriter Co. Inc., ¾" x 2½", $1.00 – 25.00. Courtesy of Tom & Mary Lou Slike.

Pegasus made in England, ¾" x 2½", $25.00 – 50.00. Courtesy of Bob & Sherri Copeland.

Penlawn by McLellan Stores Co., New York, New York, ¾" x 2½" x 2½", $1.00 – 25.00. Courtesy of Tom & Mary Lou Slike.

Personality marked Exchange Typewriter Shop, New York City, ¾" x 2½", $25.00 – 50.00. Courtesy of Tom & Mary Lou Slike.

Pigeon by Corona Typewriter Co. Inc., ¾" x 1¾" x 1¾", left & center: $1.00 – 25.00 ea.; right: $25.00 – 50.00. Courtesy of Tom & Mary Lou Slike.

Pilot Brand by Chicago Manifold Products Co., Chicago, Illinois, ¾" x 2½", $50.00 – 75.00. Courtesy of Tom & Mary Lou Slike.

Plenty Copy by Mittag & Volger Inc., Park Ridge, New Jersey, ¾" x 2½", $1.00 – 25.00. Courtesy of Tom & Mary Lou Slike.

Plenty Copy by Mittag & Volger Inc., Park Ridge, New Jersey, ¾" x 2½", $25.00 – 50.00. Courtesy of Tom & Mary Lou Slike.

Popular Quality marked Old Dutch Carbon & Ribbon Co., and Waters & Waters, Burlington, New Jersey, ¾" x 2½" x 2½", $25.00 – 50.00. Courtesy of Tom & Mary Lou Slike.

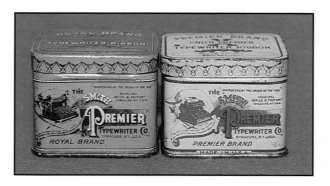

Premier by The Smith Premier Typewriter Co., Syracuse, New York, marked H.L. Hudson & Co., Brooklyn, New York, 1¾" x 2" x 1¾", $100.00 – 150.00 ea. Courtesy of Tom & Mary Lou Slike.

Princess Brand by Iowa-Frye Co., Des Moines, Iowa, ¾" x 2½" x 2½", $150.00 – 200.00. Courtesy of Hoby & Nancy Van Deusen.

Protype by Phillips Process Co., Rochester, New York, ¾" x 2½" x 2½", $1.00 – 25.00. Courtesy of Tom & Mary Lou Slike.

Puritana by The Thompson Co., Minneapolis, Minnesota, ¾" x 2½" x 2½", $25.00 – 50.00.

Pyramid by Miller-Davis Co., Minneapolis, Minnesota, ¾" x 2½", $75.00 – 100.00. Courtesy of Tom & Mary Lou Slike.

Quality stock tin, ¾" x 2½", $25.00 – 50.00.

Queen by Queen Ribbon & Carbon Co. Inc., ¾" x 2½", left: $1.00 – 25.00; center: $25.00 – 50.00; right: $1.00 – 25.00. Courtesy of Tom & Mary Lou Slike.

Raven Brand by Raven Sales Co. Inc., Woodhaven, New York, ¾" x 2½", $75.00 – 100.00. Courtesy of Hoby & Nancy Van Deusen.

Red Feather by Stenno Ribbon & Carbon Mfg. Co., Portland, Oregon, ¾" x 2½", $25.00 – 50.00. Courtesy of Tom & Mary Lou Slike.

Rembrandt cardboard by Remington Rand, Middletown, Connecticut, ¾" x 2½", $25.00 – 50.00. Courtesy of Tom & Mary Lou Slike.

Remrandco cardboard by Remington Rand, Bridgeport, Connecticut, 1" x 2½", $1.00 – 25.00. Courtesy of Tom & Mary Lou Slike.

Revilo by Oliver Typewriter Co., Chicago, Illinois, ¾" x 2½" x 2½", $1.00 – 25.00. Courtesy of Tom & Mary Lou Slike.

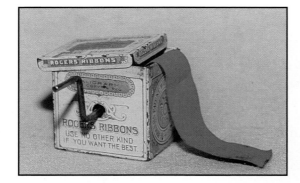

Rogers by L.H. Rogers, $350.00 – 400.00. Courtesy of Tom & Mary Lou Slike.
Note: Believed to be the first typewriter ribbon made.

Roytype by Royal Typewriter Co. Inc., New York, New York, ¾" x 2½" x 2½", $25.00 – 50.00. Courtesy of Tom & Mary Lou Slike.

Roytype Vertex by Royal Typewriter Co. Inc., New York, ¾" x 2½", $1.00 – 25.00. Courtesy of Tom & Mary Lou Slike.

Rux-Tone, manufacturer unknown, ¾" x 2½", $1.00 – 25.00. Courtesy of Tom & Mary Lou Slike.

Scout Brand by Gordon Rogers Co., Kansas City, Missouri, ¾" x 2½", $50.00 – 75.00. Courtesy of Hoby & Nancy Van Deusen.

Seal Skin by S.S. Stafford Ink Co., New York, ¾" x 2½", $200.00 – 250.00. Courtesy of Tom & Mary Lou Slike.

Service by Muncie Typewriter Exchange, Muncie, Indiana, ¾" x 2½" x 2½", showing obverse and reverse, rare, no price available. Courtesy of Wm. Morford Auctions.

Shallcross by The Shallcross Co., Philadelphia, Pennsylvania, ¾" x 2½", $25.00 – 50.00. Courtesy of Tom & Mary Lou Slike.

Silhouette, small: ¾" x 2¼"; large: ¾" x 2½"; $25.00 – 50.00 ea. Courtesy of Tom & Mary Lou Slike.

Silk cardboard by Remington Rand, Bridgeport, Connecticut, ¾" x 2½", $25.00 – 50.00. Courtesy of Tom & Mary Lou Slike.

Silk by Ault & Wiborg Co., Cincinnati, Ohio, ¾" x 2½" x 2½", $25.00 – 50.00. Courtesy of Tom & Mary Lou Slike.

Silk Spun by Mittag & Volger Inc., Park Ridge, New Jersey, ¾" x 2½", $1.00 – 25.00. Courtesy of Tom & Mary Lou Slike.

Silk-Spun by Mittag & Volger Inc., Park Ridge, New Jersey, ¾" x 2½", $25.00 – 50.00. Courtesy of Tom & Mary Lou Slike.

Silver Medal by Stenno Ribbon & Carbon Mfg. Co., Portland, Oregon, ¾" x 2½", $1.00 – 25.00. Courtesy of Tom & Mary Lou Slike.

So-Klean by Downes & Co., New York City, ¾" x 2¼" x 2¼", $25.00 – 50.00. Courtesy of Tom & Mary Lou Slike.

Stafford's Improved by S.S. Stafford Inc., New York City, ¾" x 2½", $25.00 – 50.00. Courtesy of Tom & Mary Lou Slike.

Stenno Gold Medal by Stenno Ribbon & Carbon Mfg. Co., Portland, Oregon, ¾" x 2½" x 2½", $25.00 – 50.00. Courtesy of Tom & Mary Lou Slike.

Stenno Jet by Stenno Ribbon & Carbon Mfg. Co., Portland, Oregon, ¾" x 2½", $25.00 – 50.00. Courtesy of Tom & Mary Lou Slike.

Stenotype by The Stenotype Co. Inc., Indianapolis, Indiana, marked A.C. Co. 70A, ¾" x 1¾", $25.00 – 50.00. Courtesy of Tom & Mary Lou Slike.

Sundstrand adding machine ribbon by Sundstrand Adding Machine Co., Rockford, Illinois, ¾" x 2", $25.00 – 50.00. Courtesy of Tom & Mary Lou Slike.

Surry Quality by H.L. Green Co. Inc., ¾" x 2½" x 2½", $25.00 – 50.00. Courtesy of Tom & Mary Lou Slike.

Tara by American Carbon Paper Corp., Chicago, Illinois, ¾" x 2½" x 2½", $100.00 – 150.00. Courtesy of Hoby & Nancy Van Deusen.

Texas Pride by Typewriter Supply Co., Fort Worth, Texas, ¾" x 2½", $150.00 – 200.00. Courtesy of Hoby & Nancy Van Deusen.

Tru-Mark Deluxe Brand, ¾" x 2½", $25.00 – 50.00. Courtesy of Tom & Mary Lou Slike.

Typal by Old Town Ribbon & Carbon Co. Inc., Brooklyn, New York, ¾" x 2½" x 2½", $50.00 – 75.00.

Typewriter Ribbon stock tin, ¾" x 2½", $1.00 – 25.00. Courtesy of Tom & Mary Lou Slike.

Typewriter Ribbon stock tin, ¾" x 2½", $50.00 – 75.00. Courtesy of Tom & Mary Lou Slike.
Note: Three variations exist, blue, brown, and red.

*Typist*s by International Business Machines, Rochester, New York, ¾" x 2½", $50.00 – 75.00. Courtesy of Tom & Mary Lou Slike.

U.S. Brand by U.S. Typewriter Ribbon Mfg. Co., Philadelphia, Pennsylvania, ¾" x 2½", $25.00 – 50.00.

Underwood's by John Underwood & Co., 2" x 1¾" x 1¾", $75.00 – 100.00. Courtesy of Tom & Mary Lou Slike.

US by U.S. Typewriter Ribbon Mfg. Co., Philadelphia, Pennsylvania, ¾" x 2¼" x 2¼", $25.00 – 50.00. Courtesy of Tom & Mary Lou Slike.

US by Haley Ink Co., London & New York, 2" x 1¾" x 1¾", $100.00 – 150.00. Courtesy of Tom & Mary Lou Slike.

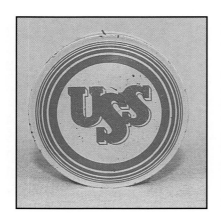

USS by United States Steel, ¾" x 2½", $25.00 – 50.00. Courtesy of Tom & Mary Lou Slike.

Vertex by Royal Typewriter Co., New York, New York, ¾" x 2½", $1.00 – 25.00. Courtesy of Tom & Mary Lou Slike.

Vivid by L.C. Smith & Corona Typewriters Inc., ¾" x 2½", $25.00 – 50.00. Courtesy of Tom & Mary Lou Slike.

Vogue by Royal Typewriter Co. Inc., New York, New York, ¾" x 2½", $1.00 – 25.00.

Write by Write Inc., New York, ¾" x 2½" x 2½", $1.00 – 25.00.

XLNT, manufacturer unknown, ¾" x 2½", $1.00 – 25.00. Courtesy of Tom & Mary Lou Slike.

MISCELLANEOUS TINS

3 Pirates prophylactic tin, 1¼" x 2" x 1½", $1,000.00 – 1,250.00. Courtesy of Wm. Morford Auctions.

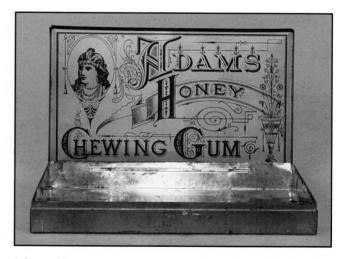

Adams Honey chewing gum by American Chicle Co., marked Ginna & Co., New York, 1" x 9" x 5½", $100.00 – 150.00. Courtesy of Hoby & Nancy Van Deusen.

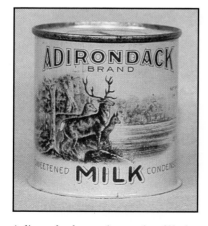

Adirondack condensed milk by Franklin County Condensed Milk Co., Bangor, New York, 3¼" x 3", $25.00 – 50.00. Courtesy of Alex & Marilyn Znaiden.

Amber Lace by Village Bath Products, Minnetonka, Minnesota, ½" x 1½", $1.00 – 25.00.

American Can Co., example tin by The American Can Co., ½" x 3¾" x 2½", $250.00 – 300.00. Courtesy of Grant Smith.

Andy Gump bank, 4½" x 3" x 1", $250.00 – 300.00. Courtesy of Wm. Morford Auctions.

Armand cold cream powder by The Armand Co., Des Moines, Iowa, ¼" x 1½", $1.00 – 25.00.

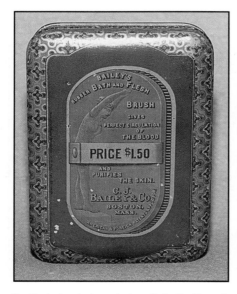

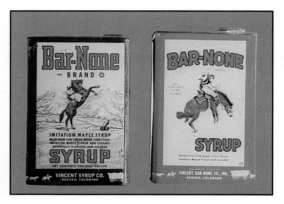

Bar-None syrup by Vincent Syrup Co., Denver Co., 7½" x 5" x 3½", left: $100.00 – 150.00; right: $75.00 – 100.00. Courtesy of Buffalo Bay Auction Co.

Bailey's bath brush by C.J. Bailey & Co., Boston, Massachusetts, marked Somers Bros., 1¼" x 3½" x 5", $100.00 – 150.00. Courtesy of Bob & Sherri Copeland.

Betsy Ross shoe polish by Black Cat Polish Co., Buffalo, New York, 1" x 3", $1.00 – 25.00. Courtesy of Alex & Marilyn Znaiden.

Big Sioux biscuit line by Manchester Biscuit Co., Sioux Falls, South Dakota & Fargo, North Dakota, $100.00 – 150.00. Courtesy of Buffalo Bay Auction Co.

Blondie paints by the American Crayon Co., Sandusky, Ohio & New York, New York, ½" x 5½" x 4½", $25.00 – 50.00. Courtesy of Tom & Lynne Sankiewicz.

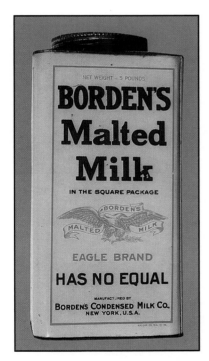

Borden's malted milk by Borden's Condensed Milk Co., New York, 10" x 4½" x 4½", $75.00 – 100.00. Courtesy of Buffalo Bay Auction Co.

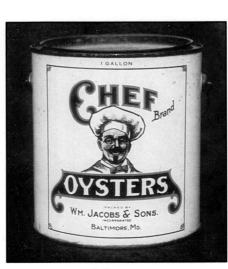

Brownie Brand peanuts by United Fig & Date Co., Chicago & New York, marked A.C. Co. 70A, 9" x 8¼", $150.00 – 200.00. Courtesy of Bob & Sherri Copeland.

Camphor Ice for by Riker Laboratories Division of United Drug Co., Boston, Massachusetts, 3½" x 1", $1.00 – 25.00. Courtesy of David Morris.

Chef oysters by Wm. Jacobs & Sons, Baltimore, Maryland, 7½" x 6½", $500.00 – 600.00. Courtesy of Alex & Marilyn Znaiden.

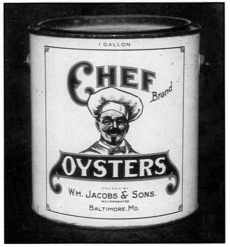

Cow Brand baking soda, ½ pound, $75.00 – 100.00. Courtesy of Buffalo Bay Auction Co.

CPC cold cream by California Perfume Co., New York, ¾" x 1½", $1.00 – 25.00.

Crystallized Canton Ginger by S.S. Pierce Co., Imported, Boston, Massachusetts, 1" x 4" x 2½", $50.00 – 75.00. Courtesy of Grant Smith.

Dayton peanut tin by Dayton Nut Products Co., Dayton, Ohio, 8¼" x 7", $350.00 – 400.00. Courtesy of Wm. Morford Auctions.

Denco dust cloth by Dennen Co., Alameda, California, 5" x 3½" x 1¾", $150.00 – 200.00. Courtesy of Wm. Morford Auction.

Desert Gold dates paper label by California Date Growers Assn., 2½" x 5", $25.00 – 50.00. Courtesy of Bob & Sherri Copeland.

Donald Duck paint box, ½" x 4½" x 3½", $50.00 – 75.00. Courtesy of Buffalo Bay Auction Co.

Dorward's Golden Star cough drops by Geo. F. Dorward, Slatington, Pennsylvania, 5 pounds, $200.00 – 250.00. Courtesy of Buffalo Bay Auctions.

Douglass & Sons cough drops marked Ginna & Co., 1½" x 4" x 2½", $75.00 – 100.00. Courtesy of Mike & Sharon Hunt.

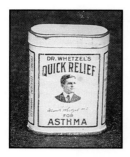

Dr. Whetzel's Quick Relief
sample by Frank Whetzel
M.D., Chicago, marked
A.C. Co. 70A, 2" x 1½" x
¾", $50.00 – 75.00. Courtesy
of Bob & Sherri Copeland.

Dustdown by The Fitch Dustdown Co., marked Heekin
Can Co., 8½" x 5¼", $75.00 –
100.00. Courtesy of Tom & Mary Lou
Slike.

Eagle Brand polish by The American
Shoe Polish Co., New York, ¾" x 2¼",
$25.00 – 50.00. Courtesy of Alex & Marilyn
Znaiden.

Eclipse tire repair kit, ½" x 3½" x 2½",
$75.00 – 100.00. Courtesy of Grant Smith.

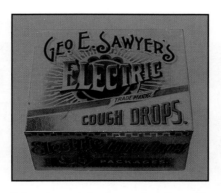

Electric cough drops by Geo. E.
Sawyer, Portland, Maine, marked
Ginna & Co., 4¼" x 8½" x 7¼",
$300.00 – 350.00. Courtesy of Wm. Morford
Auctions.

Ex-Lax laxative by Ex-Lax Inc.,
Brooklyn, New York, ¼" x 1¾" x
1¾", $1.00 – 25.00.

Expello No. 5 by Hudson
Dunaway Corp., Dover,
New Hampshire, 2" x
3½", $1.00 – 25.00. Courtesy
of David Morris.

Falcon leather polish by
J.K. Krieg & Co., New
York, ¾" x 1¾", $1.00 –
25.00. Courtesy of Alex & Marilyn
Znaiden.

Gem lighter fluid by Consolidated Royal Chemical Corp., Chicago, 5¾" x 2¼" x 1¼", $75.00 – 100.00. Courtesy of Lawson & Lin Veasey.

Giant salted peanuts by Superior Peanut Co., Cleveland, Ohio, 11" x 7½", $200.00 – 250.00. Courtesy of Richard & Ann Lehmann.

Goodrich repair kit by The B.F. Goodrich Co., Akron, Ohio, 2" x 6½" x 2½", $50.00 – 75.00. Courtesy of Tom & Lynne Sankiewicz.

Goodyear No. 6 by The Goodyear Rubber Co., New York, marked Somers Bros., 2½" x 5" x 5", $25.00 – 50.00. Courtesy of Bob & Sherri Copeland.

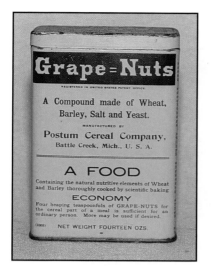

Grape-Nuts by Postum Cereal Co., Battle Creek, Michigan, 5¾" x 4" x 2", $1.00 – 25.00. Courtesy of David Morris & Steve Turner.

Gree-Soff by Thomas Paint Co., Waverly, New York, 5¼" x 6¼", $200.00 – 250.00. Courtesy of Wm. Morford Auctions.

Happer polisher & burnisher by C.H. Happer & Co., Findlay, Ohio, 6" x 2", $25.00 – 50.00. Courtesy of Bob & Sherri Copeland.

Heekin Cans lithography example give-a-way, by Heekin Can Co., Cincinnati, Ohio, 1¾" x 5" x 3½", $50.00 – 75.00.

Honey by Lorne Shelly, Tpoy, Ontario, Canada, 5" x 5", $1.00 – 25.00. Courtesy of Mitch Morganstern.

Hygieia crayons by American Crayon Co., Sandusky, Ohio & New York, New York, 3½" x 6" x 4", $1.00 – 25.00. Courtesy of Hoby & Nancy Van Deusen.

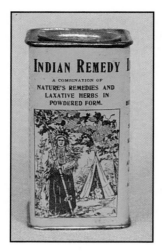

Indian Remedy laxative by Anthony Fischer Co., Salt Lake City, Utah, 3½" x 1¾" x 1¾", $75.00 – 100.00. Courtesy of Alex & Marilyn Znaiden.

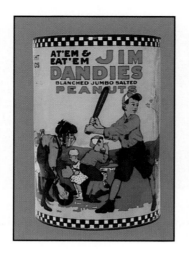

Jim Dandies peanut tin, 11" x 7½", $1,000.00 – 1,250.00.
Courtesy of Wm. Morford Auctions.

Johnson's floor wax by S.C. Johnson & Son, Racine, Wisconsin, left: 6¾" x 3"; right: 5¼" x 2½"; $50.00 – 75.00 ea.
Courtesy of Hoby & Nancy Van Deusen.

Kaola cocoanut butter, 7" x 8", $75.00 – 100.00. Courtesy of Buffalo Bay Auction Co.

Kellogg's asthma remedy by Northrop & Lyman Co. Ltd., Toronto, Canada, 5" x 2½" x 1¾", $150.00 – 200.00. Courtesy of Bob & Sherri Copeland.

Kettle rendered lard by Herman Jahn Sons Co., Marietta, Ohio, 8½" x 8", $25.00 – 50.00. Courtesy of Mitch Morganstern.

Kickapoo salve by The Kickapoo Indian Medicine Co. Inc., ½" x 2", $50.00 – 75.00. Courtesy of Alex & Marilyn Znaiden.

King-Menthol by King Manufacturing, Pittsburgh, Pennsylvania, 1" x 2½", $75.00 – 100.00. Courtesy of Grant Smith.

Klinzmoth by Klinzmoth Chemical Corp., New York & Chicago, 6" x 3", $1.00 – 25.00. Courtesy of Hoby & Nancy Van Deusen.

Liberty Brand lard by Roberts & Oake, Chicago, Illinois, 6½" x 7½", $75.00 – 100.00.

Lions stock remedy by Live Stock Remedy Co., St. Louis, Missouri, 10½" x 9¼", $150.00 – 200.00. Courtesy of Wm. Morford Auctions.

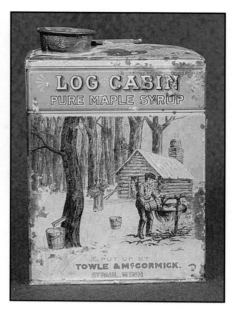

Linseed Licorice & Chlorodyne, pictures Warwick Castle, 7" x 4", $75.00 – 100.00. Courtesy of Buffalo Bay Auctions Co.

Log Cabin syrup paper label by Towle & McCormick, St. Paul, Minnesota, 6½" x 4¼" x 2¾", $200.00 – 250.00. Courtesy of Lawson & Lin Veasey.

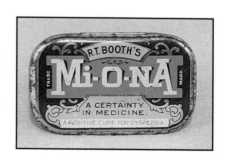

Mi-O-Na cure for dyspepsia by R.T. Booth Co., ½" x 3" x 1¾", $1.00 – 25.00. Courtesy of Bob & Sherri Copeland.

Mac Marr evaporated milk paper label by Mac Marr Stores, 3¾" x 3", $25.00 – 50.00. Courtesy of Mike & Sharon Hunt.

Madeira cough drops by E.J. Hoadley, Hartford, Connecticut, marked Somers Bros., Brooklyn, New York, 8" x 5" x 5", $1,000.00 – 1,250.00. Courtesy of Alex & Marilyn Znaiden.

Montauk oysters by Montauk Seafood Co. Inc., Fulton Market, New York, 7½" x 6½", $50.00 – 75.00. Courtesy of Buffalo Bay Auction Co.

Mother Hubbard pancack flour, cardboard with tin top and bottom by Hubbard Milling Co., Mankato, Minnesota, 9¼" x 6" x 4", $50.00 – 75.00. Courtesy of Richard & Ann Lehmann.

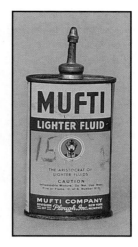

Mufti lighter fluid by Mufti Co. Division of Plough Inc., 5" x 2¼" x 1¼", $50.00 – 75.00. Courtesy of Lawson & Lin Veasey.

N.B. & C. dancing wax by Noyes Bros., St. Paul, Minnesota, 7" x 3", $100.00 – 150.00. Courtesy of Hoby & Nancy Van Deusen.

Nelson's hair dressing free sample by Nelson Manufacturing Co. Inc., Richmond, Virginia, ½" x 2" x 1", $25.00 – 50.00. Courtesy of Tom & Lynne Sankiewicz.

Niagra leather polish marked Frank Viesel Can Co., Chicago, ¾" x 1¾", $1.00 – 25.00. Courtesy of Alex & Marilyn Znaiden.

257

Nobel Glasgow blasting caps by Alfred Nobel, Australia, 1½" x 2¾" x 2¼", $75.00 – 100.00.

Old Manse syrup by Oelerich & Berry Co., marked A.C. Co. 70A, 8" x 3¾" x 2½", $25.00 – 50.00. Courtesy of Tom & Mary Lou Slike.

Oriental Brand crystallized ginger by Ruykhaver Bros., Jersey City, New Jersey, 1" x 4" x 2½", $25.00 – 50.00. Courtesy of Grant Smith.

Oriental Pot-Pourri, manufacturer unknown, 4" x 2¼" x 2¼", $25.00 – 50.00. Courtesy of Hoby & Nancy Van Deusen.

Pennant store bin with glass front by Felber Biscuit Co., Columbus, Ohio, $50.00 – 75.00.

Pepsin gum by Zeno Mfg. Co., Chicago, Illinois, ¾" x 3¼" x 1", $50.00 – 75.00. Courtesy of Bob & Sherri Copeland.

Peter Pan bread advertising bank, cardboard with tin top and bottom, 2" x 2¼" x 1", $25.00 – 50.00. Courtesy of Lawson & Lin Veasey.

Peters Weatherbird shoe advertising bank, cardboard with tin top and bottom by F.L. Rand Co., St. Louis, 2" x 1¾" x 1¼", $50.00 – 75.00. Courtesy of Lawson & Lin Veasey.

Player peanuts by Miller Peanut Products Co., Detroit, Michigan, 9½" x 8¼", $500.00 – 600.00. Courtesy of Wm. Morford Auctions.

Poll-Parrot advertising bank, cardboard with tin top and bottom by F.L. Rand Co., St. Louis, 2" x 1¾" x 1¼", $50.00 – 75.00. Courtesy of Lawson & Lin Veasey.

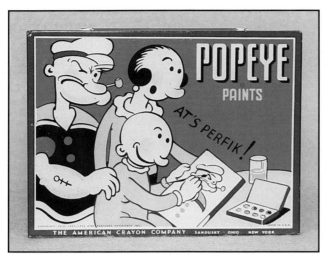

Popeye paints by The American Crayon Co., Sandusky, Ohio & New York, New York, ½" x 5½" x 4½", $25.00 – 50.00. Courtesy of Tom & Lynne Sankiewicz.

Powow cleanser sample cardboard with tin top and bottom by West Coast Soap Co., Oakland, California, 3¼" x 2", $75.00 – 100.00. Courtesy of Mike & Sharon Hunt.

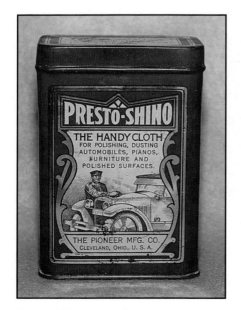

Presto-Shino polishing cloth by The Pioneer Mfg. Co., Cleveland, Ohio, 5" x 3¼" x 2", $100.00 – 150.00. Courtesy of Bob & Sherri Copeland.

Purity Brand MLB sugar butter by E.E. Post Co., Utica, New York, 3½" x 4½", $25.00 – 50.00. Courtesy of Hoby & Nancy Van Deusen.

Rat-Chips exterminator by The Rat-Chip Co.,
Dresden, Ohio, 1¾" x 3" x 3", $1.00 – 25.00.
Courtesy of Alex & Marilyn Znaiden.

Red Goose advertising bank, cardboard
with tin top and bottom by F.L. Rand Co.,
St. Louis, 2" x 1¾" x 1¼", $25.00 – 50.00.
Courtesy of Lawson & Lin Veasey.

Riley billard chalk tin by E.J. Riley
Ltd., 3" x 2" x 1", $75.00 – 100.00.
Courtesy of Buffalo Bay Auction Co.

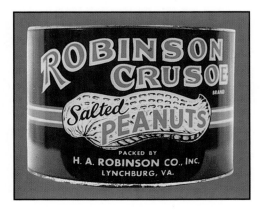

Robinson Crusoe peanuts by H.A. Robinson Co.
Inc., Lynchburg, Virginia, $100.00 – 150.00.
Courtesy of Buffalo Bay Auction Co.

Rose Leaf pot-pourri marked Somers Bros., Brooklyn, New York, 3" x 2¼" x 2¼", $50.00 – 75.00.
Courtesy of Hoby & Nancy Van Deusen.

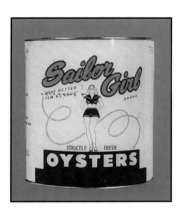

Sailor Girl oysters, 7½" x 6½", $25.00 – 50.00.
Courtesy of Buffalo Bay Auction Co.

Schlotterbeck's solvent by Schlotterbeck & Foss Manufacturing Chemist, Portland, Maine, $150.00 – 200.00. Courtesy of Grant Smith.

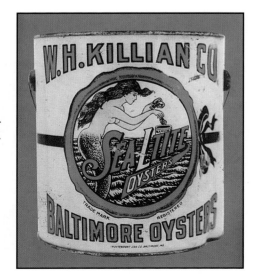

Sea-L-Tite oysters by W.H. Killian Co., Baltimore, Maryland, 7½" x 6½", $250.00 – 300.00.
Courtesy of Buffalo Bay Auction Co.

Seabury's bunion plaster by Seabury & Johnson, New York, ½" x 3" x 2¼", $50.00 – 75.00. Courtesy of Grant Smith.

Seabury's corn plaster by Seabury & Johnson, New York, ½" x 3" x 2", $50.00 – 75.00. Courtesy of Grant Smith.

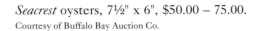

Seacrest oysters, 7½" x 6", $50.00 – 75.00. Courtesy of Buffalo Bay Auction Co.

Shawmut fuses by The Chase-Shawmut Co., Newburyport, Massachusetts, ¼" x 1¾" x 1¼", $25.00 – 50.00. Courtesy of Tom & Lynne Sankiewicz.

Silver Gem chewing gum by Sibley & Holmwood, Buffalo, New York, 2" x 7½" x 5", $100.00 – 150.00. Courtesy of Hoby & Nancy Van Deusen.

Spotlight lighter fluid by York Pharmacal Co., St. Louis, Missouri, 6" x 2" x 1¼", $25.00 – 50.00. Courtesy of Lawson & Lin Veasey.

Spry shortening by Lever Bros. Co., Cambridge, Massachusetts, $1.00 – 25.00.

Star Maid salted peanuts by The Brundage Bros. Co., Toledo, Ohio, 11" x 7½", $200.00 – 250.00. Courtesy of Richard & Ann Lehmann.

Sunbeam crystallized ginger by Austin, Nichols & Co. Inc., New York, 1" x 4" x 2½", $50.00 – 75.00. Courtesy of Grant Smith.

Sweet Georgia Brown hair dressing by Valmor Products Co., Chicago, Illinois, ¼" x 1¼", $1.00 – 25.00.

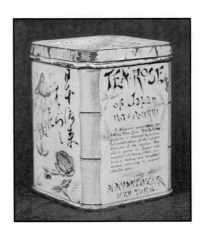

Tea Rose pot-pourri by A.A. Vantine & Co., New York, marked Somers Bros., Brooklyn, New York, 4" x 2¾", $25.00 – 50.00. Courtesy of Hoby & Nancy Van Deusen.

The Lady's Own toilet pin box by Tubbs Louis & Co. Ltd., London, Wotton, England, 1" x 3" x 2¼", $1.00 – 25.00. Courtesy of Grant Smith.

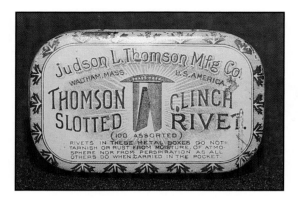

Thomson rivet by Judson L. Thomson Mfg. Co., Waltham, Massachusetts, marked Hasker & Marcuse (pre-1901), ½" x 3" x 2", $1.00 – 25.00.

Tropical Brand crystallized ginger, 1" x 4" x 2½", $25.00 – 50.00. Courtesy of Grant Smith.

Twin Brothers buggy axle grease by Crystal Oil Co., Cincinnati, Ohio, $25.00 – 50.00. Courtesy of Alex & Marilyn Znaiden.

Uncle Sam shoe polish by Yankee Polish Co., New York, ¾" x 2¼", $25.00 – 50.00. Courtesy of Alex & Marilyn Znaiden.

Vicks sample by Vick Chemical Co., Greensburg, North Carolina, ¼" x 1½", $1.00 – 25.00.

Velvet ice cream by Velvet Ice Cream, Utica, Ohio, 5" x 4¼", $1.00 – 25.00.

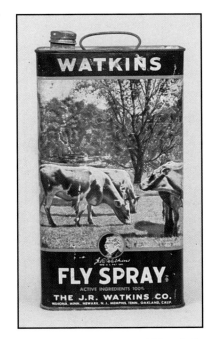

Well's Tablets laxative by The National Drug Co., Washington, D.C., ½" x 3" x 2", $1.00 – 25.00.

Watkins fly spray by The J.R. Watkins Co., marked Canco, 11½" x 6" x 4", $25.00 – 50.00.
Courtesy of Hoby & Nancy Van Deusen.

What Is It insectine by Vil-
vette Mfg. Co., Philadelphia,
Pennsylvania, 5" x 2½",
$25.00 – 50.00. Courtesy of Hoby
& Nancy Van Deusen.

Whiz Motor Rythm by R.M. Holing-
shead Corp., Camden, New Jersey,
3" x 3½", $25.00 – 50.00.

Yucatan gum by American Chicle Co., 6" x 6¾" x
4¾", $350.00 – 400.00. Courtesy of Buffalo Bay Auction Co.

Zeno chewing gum by Zeno Mfg. Co., Chicago, Illinois, 2¼"
x 9¼" x 4½", $100.00 – 150.00. Courtesy of Hoby & Nancy Van Deusen.

Antique Tins

Identification & Values   Books I & II

by Fred Dodge

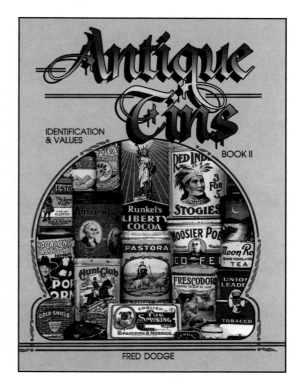

More than 3,000 different tins pictured in the two books.

Additional listings, with values, for tins not pictured.

Descriptions and measurements given for pictured tins.

Categories from tobacco, coffee and spices, to toiletries and pharmaceuticals.

Book I, 1997 values, 296 pgs., $24.95; Book II, 1998 values, 304 pgs., $29.95.

These beautiful value guides each feature over 1,500 gorgeous color photos of every type of tin. They provide current price ranges for every tin pictured, information on tin collector's clubs, and condition comparison scales. Book II also includes helpful tips for purchasing and caring for tins and information on advertising collectible clubs.

COLLECTOR BOOKS
A Division of Schroeder Publishing Co., Inc.

COLLECTOR BOOKS

Informing Today's Collector

For over two decades we have been keeping collectors informed on trends and values in all fields of antiques and collectibles.

DOLLS, FIGURES & TEDDY BEARS

4707	A Decade of **Barbie** Dolls & Collectibles, 1981–1991, Summers	$19.95
4631	**Barbie** Doll Boom, 1986–1995, Augustyniak	$18.95
2079	**Barbie** Doll Fashion, Volume I, Eames	$24.95
4846	**Barbie** Doll Fashion, Volume II, Eames	$24.95
3957	**Barbie** Exclusives, Rana	$18.95
4632	**Barbie** Exclusives, Book II, Rana	$18.95
4557	**Barbie,** The First 30 Years, Deutsch	$24.95
4847	**Barbie** Years, 1959–1995, 2nd Ed., Olds	$17.95
3310	**Black Dolls,** 1820–1991, Perkins	$17.95
3873	**Black Dolls,** Book II, Perkins	$17.95
3810	**Chatty Cathy Dolls,** Lewis	$15.95
1529	Collector's Encyclopedia of **Barbie** Dolls, DeWein	$19.95
4882	Collector's Encyclopedia of **Barbie** Doll Exclusives and More, Augustyniak	$19.95
2211	Collector's Encyclopedia of **Madame Alexander Dolls,** Smith	$24.95
4863	Collector's Encyclopedia of **Vogue Dolls,** Izen/Stover	$29.95
3967	Collector's Guide to **Trolls,** Peterson	$19.95
4571	**Liddle Kiddles,** Identification & Value Guide, Langford	$18.95
1513	Story of **Barbie,** Westenhouser	$19.95
1513	**Teddy Bears & Steiff** Animals, Mandel	$9.95
1817	**Teddy Bears & Steiff** Animals, 2nd Series, Mandel	$19.95
2084	**Teddy Bears, Annalee's & Steiff** Animals, 3rd Series, Mandel	$19.95
1808	Wonder of **Barbie,** Manos	$9.95
1430	World of **Barbie** Dolls, Manos	$9.95
4880	World of **Raggedy Ann** Collectibles, Avery	$24.95

TOYS, MARBLES & CHRISTMAS COLLECTIBLES

3427	**Advertising Character** Collectibles, Dotz	$17.95
2333	Antique & Collector's **Marbles,** 3rd Ed., Grist	$9.95
3827	Antique & Collector's **Toys,** 1870–1950, Longest	$24.95
3956	Baby Boomer **Games,** Identification & Value Guide, Polizzi	$24.95
4934	**Breyer Animal** Collector's Guide, Identification and Values, Browell	$19.95
3717	**Christmas** Collectibles, 2nd Edition, Whitmyer	$24.95
4976	**Christmas** Ornaments, Lights & Decorations, Johnson	$24.95
4737	**Christmas** Ornaments, Lights & Decorations, Vol. II, Johnson	$24.95
4739	**Christmas** Ornaments, Lights & Decorations, Vol. III, Johnson	$24.95
4649	Classic Plastic **Model Kits,** Polizzi	$24.95
4559	Collectible **Action Figures,** 2nd Ed., Manos	$17.95
3874	Collectible Coca-Cola Toy **Trucks,** deCourtivron	$24.95
2338	Collector's Encyclopedia of **Disneyana,** Longest, Stern	$24.95
4958	Collector's Guide to **Battery Toys,** Hultzman	$19.95
4639	Collector's Guide to **Diecast Toys & Scale Models,** Johnson	$19.95
4651	Collector's Guide to **Tinker Toys,** Strange	$18.95
4566	Collector's Guide to **Tootsietoys,** 2nd Ed., Richter	$19.95
4720	The Golden Age of **Automotive Toys,** 1925–1941, Hutchison/Johnson	$24.95
3436	Grist's Big Book of **Marbles**	$19.95
3970	Grist's Machine-Made & Contemporary **Marbles,** 2nd Ed.	$9.95
4723	**Matchbox** Toys, 1947 to 1996, 2nd Ed., Johnson	$18.95
4871	**McDonald's Collectibles,** Henriques/DuVall	$19.95
1540	**Modern Toys** 1930–1980, Baker	$19.95
3888	**Motorcycle** Toys, Antique & Contemporary, Gentry/Downs	$18.95
4953	Schroeder's Collectible **Toys,** Antique to Modern Price Guide, 4th Ed.	$17.95
1886	Stern's Guide to **Disney** Collectibles	$14.95
2139	Stern's Guide to **Disney** Collectibles, 2nd Series	$14.95
3975	Stern's Guide to **Disney** Collectibles, 3rd Series	$18.95
2028	**Toys,** Antique & Collectible, Longest	$14.95
3979	**Zany Characters** of the Ad World, Lamphier	$16.95

FURNITURE

1457	American **Oak** Furniture, McNerney	$9.95
3716	American **Oak** Furniture, Book II, McNerney	$12.95
1118	Antique **Oak** Furniture, Hill	$7.95
2271	Collector's Encyclopedia of **American** Furniture, Vol. II, Swedberg	$24.95
3720	Collector's Encyclopedia of **American** Furniture, Vol. III, Swedberg	$24.95
3878	Collector's Guide to **Oak** Furniture, George	$12.95
1755	Furniture of the **Depression Era,** Swedberg	$19.95
3906	**Heywood-Wakefield** Modern Furniture, Rouland	$18.95

1885	**Victorian** Furniture, Our American Heritage, McNerney	$9.95
3829	**Victorian** Furniture, Our American Heritage, Book II, McNerney	$9.95

JEWELRY, HATPINS, WATCHES & PURSES

1712	Antique & Collector's **Thimbles** & Accessories, Mathis	$19.95
1748	Antique **Purses,** Revised Second Ed., Holiner	$19.95
1278	Art Nouveau & Art Deco **Jewelry,** Baker	$9.95
4850	Collectible **Costume Jewelry,** Simonds	$24.95
3875	Collecting Antique **Stickpins,** Kerins	$16.95
3722	Collector's Ency. of **Compacts, Carryalls & Face Powder Boxes,** Mueller	$24.95
4854	Collector's Ency. of **Compacts, Carryalls & Face Powder Boxes,** Vol. II	$24.95
4940	**Costume Jewelry,** A Practical Handbook & Value Guide, Rezazadeh	$24.95
1716	Fifty Years of Collectible **Fashion Jewelry,** 1925–1975, Baker	$19.95
1424	**Hatpins** & Hatpin Holders, Baker	$9.95
4570	Ladies' **Compacts,** Gerson	$24.95
1181	100 Years of Collectible **Jewelry,** 1850–1950, Baker	$9.95
4729	**Sewing Tools** & Trinkets, Thompson	$24.95
2348	20th Century Fashionable Plastic **Jewelry,** Baker	$19.95
4878	Vintage & Contemporary **Purse Accessories,** Gerson	$24.95
3830	Vintage **Vanity Bags & Purses,** Gerson	$24.95

INDIANS, GUNS, KNIVES, TOOLS, PRIMITIVES

1868	Antique **Tools,** Our American Heritage, McNerney	$9.95
1426	**Arrowheads** & Projectile Points, Hothem	$7.95
4943	Field Guide to **Flint Arrowheads & Knives** of the North American Indian	$9.95
2279	**Indian Artifacts** of the Midwest, Hothem	$14.95
3885	**Indian Artifacts** of the Midwest, Book II, Hothem	$16.95
4870	**Indian Artifacts** of the Midwest, Book III, Hothem	$18.95
1964	**Indian Axes** & Related Stone Artifacts, Hothem	$14.95
2023	**Keen Kutter** Collectibles, Heuring	$14.95
4724	Modern **Guns,** Identification & Values, 11th Ed., Quertermous	$12.95
2164	**Primitives,** Our American Heritage, McNerney	$9.95
1759	**Primitives,** Our American Heritage, 2nd Series, McNerney	$14.95
4730	Standard **Knife** Collector's Guide, 3rd Ed., Ritchie & Stewart	$12.95

PAPER COLLECTIBLES & BOOKS

4633	**Big Little Books,** Jacobs	$18.95
4710	Collector's Guide to **Children's Books,** Jones	$18.95
1441	Collector's Guide to **Post Cards,** Wood	$9.95
2081	Guide to Collecting **Cookbooks,** Allen	$14.95
2080	Price Guide to **Cookbooks & Recipe Leaflets,** Dickinson	$9.95
3973	**Sheet Music** Reference & Price Guide, 2nd Ed., Pafik & Guiheen	$19.95
4654	**Victorian Trade Cards,** Historical Reference & Value Guide, Cheadle	$19.95
4733	**Whitman Juvenile Books,** Brown	$17.95

GLASSWARE

4561	Collectible **Drinking Glasses,** Chase & Kelly	$17.95
4642	Collectible **Glass Shoes,** Wheatley	$19.95
4937	Coll. **Glassware from the 40s, 50s & 60s,** 4th Ed., Florence	$19.95
1810	Collector's Encyclopedia of **American Art Glass,** Shuman	$29.95
4938	Collector's Encyclopedia of **Depression Glass,** 13th Ed., Florence	$19.95
1961	Collector's Encyclopedia of **Fry Glassware,** Fry Glass Society	$24.95
1664	Collector's Encyclopedia of **Heisey Glass,** 1925–1938, Bredehoft	$24.95
3905	Collector's Encyclopedia of **Milk Glass,** Newbound	$24.95
4936	Collector's Guide to **Candy Containers,** Dezso/Poirier	$19.95
4564	**Crackle Glass,** Weitman	$19.95
4941	**Crackle Glass,** Book II, Weitman	$19.95
2275	**Czechoslovakian Glass** and Collectibles, Barta/Rose	$16.95
4714	**Czechoslovakian Glass** and Collectibles, Book II, Barta/Rose	$16.95
4716	**Elegant Glassware** of the Depression Era, 7th Ed., Florence	$19.95
1380	Encyclopedia of **Pattern Glass,** McClain	$12.95
3981	Ever's Standard **Cut Glass** Value Guide	$12.95
4659	**Fenton** Art Glass, 1907–1939, Whitmyer	$24.95
3725	**Fostoria,** Pressed, Blown & Hand Molded Shapes, Kerr	$24.95
4719	**Fostoria,** Etched, Carved & Cut Designs, Vol. II, Kerr	$24.95
3883	**Fostoria Stemware,** The Crystal for America, Long & Seate	$24.95
4644	**Imperial Carnival Glass,** Burns	$18.95
3886	**Kitchen Glassware** of the Depression Years, 5th Ed., Florence	$19.95

4725	Pocket Guide to **Depression Glass**, 10th Ed., Florence	$9.95
5035	Standard Encyclopedia of **Carnival Glass**, 6th Ed., Edwards/Carwile	$24.95
5036	Standard **Carnival Glass** Price Guide, 11th Ed., Edwards/Carwile	$9.95
4875	Standard Encyclopedia of **Opalescent Glass**, 2nd ed., Edwards	$19.95
4731	**Stemware Identification**, Featuring Cordials with Values, Florence	$24.95
3326	**Very Rare Glassware** of the Depression Years, 3rd Series, Florence	$24.95
4732	**Very Rare Glassware** of the Depression Years, 5th Series, Florence	$24.95
4656	**Westmoreland Glass**, Wilson	$24.95

POTTERY

4927	**ABC Plates & Mugs**, Lindsay	$24.95
4929	**American Art Pottery**, Sigafoose	$24.95
4630	**American Limoges**, Limoges	$24.95
1312	**Blue & White Stoneware**, McNerney	$9.95
1958	So. Potteries **Blue Ridge Dinnerware**, 3rd Ed., Newbound	$14.95
1959	**Blue Willow**, 2nd Ed., Gaston	$14.95
4848	Ceramic **Coin Banks**, Stoddard	$19.95
4851	Collectible **Cups & Saucers**, Harran	$18.95
4709	Collectible **Kay Finch**, Biography, Identification & Values, Martinez/Frick	$18.95
1373	Collector's Encyclopedia of **American Dinnerware**, Cunningham	$24.95
4931	Collector's Encyclopedia of **Bauer Pottery**, Chipman	$24.95
3815	Collector's Encyclopedia of **Blue Ridge Dinnerware**, Newbound	$19.95
4932	Collector's Encyclopedia of **Blue Ridge Dinnerware**, Vol. II, Newbound	$24.95
4658	Collector's Encyclopedia of **Brush-McCoy Pottery**, Huxford	$24.95
2272	Collector's Encyclopedia of **California Pottery**, Chipman	$24.95
2133	Collector's Encyclopedia of **Colorado Pottery**, Carlton	$24.95
3811	Collector's Encyclopedia of **Cookie Jars**, Roerig	$24.95
3723	Collector's Encyclopedia of **Cookie Jars**, Book II, Roerig	$24.95
4939	Collector's Encyclopedia of **Cookie Jars**, Book III, Roerig	$24.95
4638	Collector's Encyclopedia of **Dakota Potteries**, Dommel	$24.95
5040	Collector's Encyclopedia of **Fiesta**, 8th Ed., Huxford	$19.95
4718	Collector's Encyclopedia of **Figural Planters & Vases**, Newbound	$19.95
3961	Collector's Encyclopedia of **Early Noritake**, Alden	$24.95
1439	Collector's Encyclopedia of **Flow Blue China**, Gaston	$19.95
3812	Collector's Encyclopedia of **Flow Blue China**, 2nd Ed., Gaston	$24.95
3813	Collector's Encyclopedia of **Hall China**, 2nd Ed., Whitmyer	$24.95
3431	Collector's Encyclopedia of **Homer Laughlin China**, Jasper	$24.95
1276	Collector's Encyclopedia of **Hull Pottery**, Roberts	$19.95
3962	Collector's Encyclopedia of **Lefton China**, DeLozier	$19.95
4855	Collector's Encyclopedia of **Lefton China**, Book II, DeLozier	$19.95
2210	Collector's Encyclopedia of **Limoges Porcelain**, 2nd Ed., Gaston	$24.95
2334	Collector's Encyclopedia of **Majolica Pottery**, Katz-Marks	$19.95
1358	Collector's Encyclopedia of **McCoy Pottery**, Huxford	$19.95
3963	Collector's Encyclopedia of **Metlox Potteries**, Gibbs Jr.	$24.95
3837	Collector's Encyclopedia of **Nippon Porcelain**, Van Patten	$24.95
2089	Collector's Ency. of **Nippon Porcelain**, 2nd Series, Van Patten	$24.95
1665	Collector's Ency. of **Nippon Porcelain**, 3rd Series, Van Patten	$24.95
4712	Collector's Ency. of **Nippon Porcelain**, 4th Series, Van Patten	$24.95
1447	Collector's Encyclopedia of **Noritake**, Van Patten	$19.95
3432	Collector's Encyclopedia of **Noritake**, 2nd Series, Van Patten	$24.95
1037	Collector's Encyclopedia of **Occupied Japan**, 1st Series, Florence	$14.95
1038	Collector's Encyclopedia of **Occupied Japan**, 2nd Series, Florence	$14.95
2088	Collector's Encyclopedia of **Occupied Japan**, 3rd Series, Florence	$14.95
2019	Collector's Encyclopedia of **Occupied Japan**, 4th Series, Florence	$14.95
2335	Collector's Encyclopedia of **Occupied Japan**, 5th Series, Florence	$14.95
4951	Collector's Encyclopedia of **Old Ivory China**, Hillman	$24.95
3964	Collector's Encyclopedia of **Pickard China**, Reed	$24.95
3877	Collector's Encyclopedia of **R.S. Prussia**, 4th Series, Gaston	$24.95
1034	Collector's Encyclopedia of **Roseville Pottery**, Huxford	$19.95
1035	Collector's Encyclopeida of **Roseville Pottery**, 2nd Ed., Huxford	$19.95
4856	Collector's Encyclopedia of **Russel Wright**, 2nd Ed., Kerr	$24.95
4713	Collector's Encyclopedia of **Salt Glaze Stoneware**, Taylor/Lowrance	$24.95
3314	Collector's Encyclopedia of **Van Briggle** Art Pottery, Sasicki	$24.95
4563	Collector's Encyclopedia of **Wall Pockets**, Newbound	$19.95
2111	Collector's Encyclopedia of **Weller Pottery**, Huxford	$29.95
3876	Collector's Guide to **Lu-Ray Pastels**, Meehan	$18.95
3814	Collector's Guide to **Made in Japan** Ceramics, White	$18.95
4646	Collector's Guide to **Made in Japan** Ceramics, Book II, White	$18.95
4565	Collector's Guide to **Rockingham**, The Enduring Ware, Brewer	$14.95
2339	Collector's Guide to **Shawnee Pottery**, Vanderbilt	$19.95
1425	**Cookie Jars**, Westfall	$9.95

3440	**Cookie Jars**, Book II, Westfall	$19.95
4924	Figural & Novelty **Salt & Pepper Shakers**, 2nd Series, Davern	$24.95
2379	Lehner's Ency. of **U.S. Marks** on Pottery, Porcelain & China	$24.95
4722	**McCoy Pottery**, Collector's Reference & Value Guide, Hanson/Nissen	$19.95
3825	**Purinton Pottery**, Morris	$24.95
4726	**Red Wing Art Pottery**, 1920s–1960s, Dollen	$19.95
1670	**Red Wing Collectibles**, DePasquale	$9.95
1440	**Red Wing Stoneware**, DePasquale	$9.95
1632	**Salt & Pepper Shakers**, Guarnaccia	$9.95
5091	**Salt & Pepper Shakers** II, Guarnaccia	$18.95
2220	**Salt & Pepper Shakers** III, Guarnaccia	$14.95
3443	**Salt & Pepper Shakers** IV, Guarnaccia	$18.95
3738	**Shawnee Pottery**, Mangus	$24.95
4629	Turn of the Century **American Dinnerware**, 1880s–1920s, Jasper	$24.95
4572	**Wall Pockets** of the Past, Perkins	$17.95
3327	**Watt Pottery** – Identification & Value Guide, Morris	$19.95

OTHER COLLECTIBLES

4704	Antique & Collectible **Buttons**, Wisniewski	$19.95
2269	Antique **Brass & Copper** Collectibles, Gaston	$16.95
1880	Antique **Iron**, McNerney	$9.95
3872	Antique **Tins**, Dodge	$24.95
4845	Antique **Typewriters & Office Collectibles**, Rehr	$19.95
1714	**Black** Collectibles, Gibbs	$19.95
1128	**Bottle** Pricing Guide, 3rd Ed., Cleveland	$7.95
4636	**Celluloid Collectibles**, Dunn	$14.95
3718	Collectible **Aluminum**, Grist	$16.95
3445	Collectible **Cats**, An Identification & Value Guide, Fyke	$18.95
4560	Collectible **Cats**, An Identification & Value Guide, Book II, Fyke	$19.95
4852	Collectible **Compact Disc** Price Guide 2, Cooper	$17.95
2018	Collector's Encyclopedia of **Granite Ware**, Greguire	$24.95
3430	Collector's Encyclopedia of **Granite Ware**, Book 2, Greguire	$24.95
4705	Collector's Guide to **Antique Radios**, 4th Ed., Bunis	$18.95
3880	Collector's Guide to **Cigarette Lighters**, Flanagan	$17.95
4637	Collector's Guide to **Cigarette Lighers**, Book II, Flanagan	$17.95
4942	Collector's Guide to **Don Winton Designs**, Ellis	$19.95
3966	Collector's Guide to **Inkwells**, Identification & Values, Badders	$18.95
4947	Collector's Guide to **Inkwells**, Book II, Badders	$19.95
4948	Collector's Guide to **Letter Openers**, Grist	$19.95
4862	Collector's Guide to **Toasters** & Accessories, Greguire	$19.95
4652	Collector's Guide to **Transistor Radios**, 2nd Ed., Bunis	$16.95
4653	Collector's Guide to **TV Memorabilia**, 1960s–1970s, Davis/Morgan	$24.95
4864	Collector's Guide to **Wallace Nutting Pictures**, Ivankovich	$18.95
1629	**Doorstops**, Identification & Values, Bertoia	$9.95
4567	Figural **Napkin Rings**, Gottschalk & Whitson	$18.95
4717	Figural **Nodders**, Includes Bobbin' Heads and Swayers, Irtz	$19.95
3968	**Fishing Lure** Collectibles, Murphy/Edmisten	$24.95
4867	**Flea Market Trader**, 11th Ed., Huxford	$9.95
4944	**Flue Covers**, Collector's Value Guide, Meckley	$12.95
4945	**G-Men and FBI Toys** and Collectibles, Whitworth	$18.95
5043	**Garage Sale & Flea Market Annual**, 6th Ed.	$19.95
3819	**General Store Collectibles**, Wilson	$24.95
4643	**Great American West** Collectibles, Wilson	$24.95
2215	Goldstein's **Coca-Cola** Collectibles	$16.95
3884	Huxford's Collectible **Advertising**, 2nd Ed.	$24.95
2216	**Kitchen Antiques**, 1790–1940, McNerney	$14.95
4950	The **Lone Ranger**, Collector's Reference & Value Guide, Felbinger	$18.95
2026	**Railroad** Collectibles, 4th Ed., Baker	$14.95
4949	**Schroeder's Antiques Price Guide**, 16th Ed., Huxford	$12.95
5007	**Silverplated Flatware**, Revised 4th Edition, Hagan	$18.95
1922	**Standard Old Bottle** Price Guide, Sellari	$14.95
4708	**Summers' Guide to Coca-Cola**	$19.95
4952	Summers' Pocket Guide to **Coca-Cola** Identifications	$9.95
3892	**Toy & Miniature Sewing Machines**, Thomas	$18.95
4876	**Toy & Miniature Sewing Machines**, Book II, Thomas	$24.95
3828	Value Guide to **Advertising Memorabilia**, Summers	$18.95
3977	Value Guide to **Gas Station** Memorabilia, Summers & Priddy	$24.95
4877	Vintage **Bar Ware**, Visakay	$24.95
4935	The W.F. Cody **Buffalo Bill** Collector's Guide with Values	$24.95
4879	**Wanted to Buy**, 6th Edition	$9.95